Come out, come out,
wherever you are.

GLINDA, THE GOOD WITCH

The Wizard of Oz

Prelude

Let's face it: anyone who picks up a book with the title *We Give To Love: Giving Is Such a Selfish Thing—Notes and Quotes on the Joys of Heartfelt Service* is a giver at heart. (Or is a pushover for books with long titles.)

Unfortunately, in our culture we are more conditioned to *get* than to *give*. For every Mother Teresa who becomes famous for giving, there are hundreds of "heroes" who become famous for getting—getting rich, getting awards, getting high scores, getting elected, getting married. (Even the language proclaims we "get married" rather than "give ourselves in marriage.")

We givers, then, can feel uncomfortable—sometimes *unnatural*—with our natural desire to give. Yes, getting is important to givers, but primarily so that they'll have something to give. Givers often feel out of place in a society where consuming is more important than compassion, acquiring more important than bequeathing, and amassing more important than service. Givers often "go into the closet" and hide their true natures of loving, caring, and sharing.

Givers: It's time to come out of the closet!

This book is about coming out. It's a book that says it's okay to devote a goodly portion of your life to giving, service, and kindness. This is not a book for everyone: only those who hear the call. If your desires run more toward *doing for* rather than *getting from,* you are not alone. Nor are you strange, weird, or unusual. You're just a giver.

Welcome to the club—and to "our" book.

*The love I give you
is secondhand—
I feel it first.*

*"We give to love"
has two meanings.*

*First, we give to
feel the love as we give
it.*

*Second, each time
we give, we contribute
to the great collective
pool of love which can
be used by anyone,
anytime, anywhere.*

Service, anyone?

Books by John-Roger and Peter McWilliams

You Can't Afford the Luxury of a Negative Thought: A Book for People with Any Life-Threatening Illness—Including Life

Focus on the Positive: The You Can't Afford the Luxury of a Negative Thought Workbook

LIFE 101: Everything We Wish We Had Learned About Life In School—But Didn't

The Portable LIFE 101

DO IT! Let's Get Off Our Buts

The Portable DO IT!

WEALTH 101: Wealth Is Much More Than Money

We Give To Love: Giving Is Such a Selfish Thing—Notes and Quotes on the Joys of Heartfelt Service

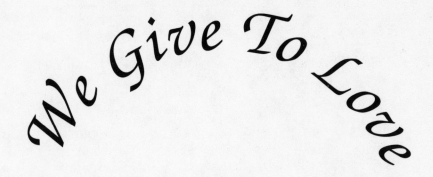

We Give To Love

Giving Is Such a Selfish Thing

NOTES AND QUOTES ON THE JOYS OF HEARTFELT SERVICE

BY

JOHN-ROGER AND PETER MCWILLIAMS

ISBN 0-931580-65-X

Editor: Jean Sedillos
Editorial Director: Chris GeRue
Desktop Publishing: Carol Taylor
Production: Paurvi Trivedi
Book and Jacket Design: Peter McWilliams and Paul LeBus
Heart-in-Hands Design: John-Roger, Ingrid Avalon
and David Jarvis
Heart-in-Hands Illustration: David Jarvis
Other Hearts: Peter McWilliams

If your local bookstore is out,
please order additional copies by calling

1–800–LIFE–101

*If there be any truer
measure of a man
than by what he does,
it must be
by what he gives.*

ROBERT SOUTH

CONTENTS

PART THREE
WE GIVE TO OTHERS

PART FOUR
WE GIVE TO FAMILY

Give your ears,
hear the sayings,
Give your heart
to understand them;
It profits to put them
in your heart.

AMENEMOPE

Eleventh Century B.C.

Get Up and Give

If at any point while reading this book you think of someone who would enjoy receiving a phone call from you; a place to go where the gift of your presence would be appreciated; or something to do that would benefit another, the world, or humanity in general; please set aside this book and call, go, do.

As often as you can, experience giving firsthand.

The lessons in giving lie in the act of giving, not reading about giving. These words are here to inspire, motivate, and encourage.

Give more in the ways that you have already given; give in ways that you have never given before.

To this end, we wrote brief chapters, making the book easy to put down. Put it down often. Go give.

As you give, take notice of what you receive.

Although this book can be read in one sitting, if we've done our job, no one will.

May you never finish this book.

*The poor don't know
that their function
in life is to exercise
our generosity.*

JEAN-PAUL SARTRE

We Give To Love

Giving Is Such a Selfish Thing

NOTES AND QUOTES ON THE JOYS
OF HEARTFELT SERVICE

*What you get
is a living—
what you give is a life.*

LILLIAN GISH

Part One

We Give to Live

*The purpose
of human life
is to serve and
to show compassion
and the will
to help others.*

ALBERT SCHWEITZER

Giving: The Purpose of Life?

We can't say giving is the purpose of *everyone's* life. Purposes are individual and personal, like fingerprints, freckles, or taste in music.

We can say, however, that if *your* purpose includes words and concepts such as "service," "giving," "sharing," "compassion," or "kindness," you will not be truly satisfied until a goodly portion of your life is given to giving.

"I don't know what your destiny will be, but one thing I know": wrote Dr. Albert Schweitzer (who knew), "the only ones among you who will be really happy are those who will have sought and found how to serve."

*The sole meaning of life
is to serve humanity.*

LEO TOLSTOI

Giving Gives Meaning

"When people are serving," wrote John Gardner, "life is no longer meaningless."

When our gift is found worthy, we feel worthy too.

This is, of course, always true—but we don't always *feel* it's true. When we give—at the very least—we are more likely to believe that our life has meaning; that we are living our life *on purpose*.

Nothing comes from nothing, so if something comes from us, we must *be* something.

This giving does not need to be Great Deeds. As Jackson Browne sang, "Sometimes the touch of a friend is enough."

"So long as we love we serve; so long as we are loved by others, I would almost say that we are indispensable," wrote Robert Louis Stevenson; "and no man is useless while he has a friend."

We find our lives in losing them in service to others.

*It's a bit embarrassing
to have been concerned
with the human problem
all one's life
and find at the end
that one has
no more to offer
by way of advice than
"Try to be a little kinder."*

ALDOUS HUXLEY

Try to Be a Little Kinder

We're not sure if the simplicity of that phrase makes it profound, or the profundity makes it simple. It is, nonetheless, what many great minds and hearts have concluded after a lifetime of discovery.

Wordsworth wrote:

> That best portion of a good man's life,
> His little, nameless, unremembered acts
> Of kindness and of love.

"My feeling is that there is nothing in life but refraining from hurting others," wrote Olive Schreiner, "and comforting those that are sad."

"Kindness in words creates confidence," taught Lao-tzu in the fifth century B.C. "Kindness in thinking creates profoundness. Kindness in giving creates love."

*Life is
a place of service,
and in that
service one has to
suffer a great deal
that is hard to bear,
but more often
to experience
a great deal of joy.*

TOLSTOI

The Courage to Give

The word *courage* comes from the French *coeur,* meaning *heart.* We need great courage (heart) to give. Service is not for sissies.

Giving is the easiest, most difficult thing you'll ever do.

In order to give, you must be willing to experience rejection and being misunderstood—not to mention the fear of rejection and the fear of being misunderstood, and the hurt of rejection and the hurt of being misunderstood, and the anger that covers the fear and the anger we turn against ourselves (guilt), and the anger and that sense of worthlessness that sometimes come when our gift is not found worthy.

In addition to pain, we must be willing to feel joy. Tolstoi (which rhymes with joy—but not very often) completes the thought he began on the facing page:

> But that joy can be real only if people look upon their life as a service, and have a definite object in life outside themselves and their personal happiness.

A hundred times
every day I remind myself
that my inner and outer life
are based on the labors
of other men,
living and dead,
and that I
must exert myself
in order to give
in the same measure
as I have received
and am still receiving.

ALBERT EINSTEIN

Service on Our Debt

We came into this life and were given much: food, language, love, the world, and the accumulated wisdom of humankind—especially VCRs.

Some look upon a portion of their giving as service on this debt. We are beholden to the past. Of course, the past doesn't need our service—but the future does. Generations yet unborn will appreciate what we have done, just as we appreciate what others—long gone—have done.

The old saying "Don't return a favor, pass it on" certainly fits. There's no way to return the favor to posterity, but we can pass it on to the future.

*This is our special duty,
that if anyone
specially needs our help,
we should give
him such help to the
utmost of our power.*

CICERO

Do Your Duty

Some consider doing for others a duty, the obligation we have to all life on this intricately interdependent planet. (If you believe you're an independent individual, please remember Carl Sagan's words: "If you want to create an apple pie from scratch, first you have to create the universe.")

The marching song for those who believe service is a duty goes something like this:

> I owe, I owe,
> It's off to give I go.

We do owe something to humanity, the earth, all life. As John D. Rockefeller, Jr., wrote:

> I believe that every right implies a responsibility; every opportunity, an obligation; every possession, a duty.

> I believe that the rendering of useful service is the common duty of mankind and that only in the purifying fire of sacrifice is the dross of selfishness consumed and the greatness of the human soul set free.

(If you serve from a sense of duty, it's okay to enjoy yourself, too. In fact, it's highly recommended. We'll discuss this in detail later.)

Service is
the rent that you pay
for room on this earth.

SHIRLEY CHISHOLM

Service is the rent
each of us pays for living—
the very purpose of life
and not something you do
in your spare time
or after you have reached
your personal goals.

MARIAN WRIGHT EDELMAN

It's the Landlord!

Some say service is the rent we pay for our space on this earth. (It's more like rent than a mortgage payment, as none of us will be here forever, so we never permanently own anything.)

If we want "2 rms riv vu," we have to pay the piper. (Actually, we have to pay the landlord—we pay the piper when we want to dance; we pay the landlord for the use of the dance floor.) If we don't want to be homeless, we pay.

The choice, of course, is the attitude with which we pay. Do we treat the landlord like a lord, or do we treat the landlord like land (dirt)?

As we shall explore shortly, the attitude with which we give is the attitude with which we receive.

The Sea of Galilee
and the Dead Sea are
made of the same water.
It flows down,
clear and cool,
from the heights of Hermon
and the roots of
the cedars of Lebanon.
The Sea of Galilee
makes beauty of it,
for the Sea of Galilee
has an outlet.
It gets to give.
It gathers in its riches that
it may pour them out again
to fertilize the Jordan plain.
But the Dead Sea with the
same water makes horror.
For the Dead Sea
has no outlet.
It gets to keep.

HARRY EMERSON FOSDICK

The Need to Give

Perhaps the most eloquent expression of our need to give was published in Harry Emerson Fosdick's 1920 book, *The Meaning of Service*. He uses an analogy from the Holy Land—rivers that run parallel to human life.

Notice especially the phrase "It gets to give." This expresses what a *privilege* it is to serve. Each time we give, we are affirming, "Thank you: I have more than I need."

Each opportunity for service should be met with gratitude. As E. A. Robinson pointed out, "There are two kinds of gratitude: The sudden kind we feel for what we take; the larger kind we feel for what we give."

*When you cease
to make a contribution,
you begin to die.*

ELEANOR ROOSEVELT

A Simple Matter of
Life and Death

Harry Emerson Fosdick's eloquence was made even simpler by Eleanor Roosevelt (who had a knack for such things).

She saw death as not just physical death (although when we withhold, that takes place, too), but the gradual dimming of our inner light, our connectedness to life, our relations with ourselves and with everyone and everything around us.

To paraphrase Mrs. Roosevelt: you begin to die the first time you are asked to give, are able to give, know it's for the highest good, and don't.

It is a slow death. Some people have it so well justified that their selfishness has become a code of honor. That is too bad. Wonder what we can do to serve them?

*A large part
of altruism,
even when it is
perfectly honest,
is grounded
upon the fact
that it is uncomfortable
to have unhappy people
about one.*

H. L. MENCKEN

Curmudgeonly Gifts

Giving is not just something goody-goody people do: some of the greatest curmudgeons of all time have acknowledged the fact that we do good *because it's good for us.*

As Mark Twain wrote toward the end of his life:

> Duties are not performed for duty's sake, but because their neglect would make the man *uncomfortable.* A man performs but *one* duty—the duty of contenting his spirit, the duty of making himself agreeable to himself.

It wouldn't be much fun to own everything in the world, while everyone else had nothing. (It would also not be politically expedient, but that's another issue altogether—or is it?)

With most people willing to give a little, the world turns a lot easier. A little giving makes a more enjoyable world, so we give—like it or not—because we *do* like living in a better world.

For example, someone may stop us and ask directions and we may not *feel* like giving directions. If *nobody ever* gave directions, however, it would be hard to get around. So, we take the time and give the directions. We prefer living in a world where it's easier to get around.

If *nobody* gave, this would be an ugly *(uglier)* world. So, not liking ugly, we give.

Besides, as Sir Philip Gibbs observed, "It's better to give than to lend, and it costs about the same." A curmudgeonly gift of humor—and truth.

*Each little thing that we do
passes into the great
machine of life which
may grind our virtues to
powder and make them
worthless,
or transform
our sins into elements
of a new civilisation,
more marvellous and
more splendid than
any that has gone before.*

OSCAR WILDE

Men are capable,
not only of fear and hate,
but also of hope
and benevolence.
If the populations of the world
can be brought to see
and to realize in imagination
the hell to which
hate and fear must condemn
them on the one hand,
and, on the other,
the comparative heaven
which hope and benevolence
can create by means
of new skills,
the choice should
not be difficult,
and our self-tormented species
should allow itself a life
of joy such as the past
has never known.

BERTRAND RUSSELL

*We are here on earth
to do good to others.
What the others
are here for,
I don't know.*

W. H. AUDEN

Needing the Needy

When we realize that our purpose is to give, we become needy. We need to fulfill our purpose, and if our purpose is to give, we need someone, something, or some cause to give to.

We need the needy. (Or, if that's too grasping, we want the wanting.)

It's an ancient idea. As Aristotle pointed out in the fourth century B.C.:

> The unfortunate need people who will be kind to them; the prosperous need people to be kind to.

As Nietzsche wrote 2,200 years later (give or take a week):

> Should not the giver be thankful that the receiver received? Is not giving a need?

This book was written for the givers. What the others are reading it for, we don't know.

*From everyone who
has been given much,
much will be demanded;
and from the one
who has been
entrusted with much,
much more
will be asked.*

JESUS OF NAZARETH

Luke 12:48

How Much Do We Give?

That depends on how much we've been given: from whom much has been given, much is expected.

Andrew Carnegie wrote:

> Surplus wealth is a sacred trust which its possessor is bound to administer in his lifetime for the good of the community.

Those who are given much—or given the gift of making much—can, if they choose, become Mondo Consumers: more houses, bigger houses; more cars, more expensive cars; boats, limos, private jets—everything the producers of "Lifestyles of the Rich and Famous" grew rich and famous dangling in front of our lustful eyes. (Didn't these people ever hear that useful bit of advice, "Thou shalt not covet thy neighbor's goods"?)

Those who have lived the life of material excess know it is not a life of luxury: it is a life of *maintenance*. A life of obtaining soon becomes a life of *maintaining*. Keeping up with the Joneses also means keeping up all that *stuff*.

"Luxury comes as a guest," as the Hindu proverb states, "and soon becomes the master."

Luckily, some who have been given much have also been given the wisdom to see that the excess (be it an excess of money, time, ability, ideas, love, humor, or anything else we possess in abundance) was given to us so that we might have the joy of giving it away.

Follow your bliss.

JOSEPH CAMPBELL

Receiving is joyful, but giving is blissful.

Whatever we've been given in abundance, inherent in that gift is the bliss of giving it away.

*As the duty is
precisely correspondent
to the power,
it follows that
the richer,
the wiser,
the more powerful
a man is,
the greater is the
obligation upon him
to employ his gifts
in lessening the sum
of human misery;
and this employment
constitutes happiness.*

JOHN RANDOLPH

1806

*Just as the wave
cannot exist for itself,
but is ever a part
of the heaving surface
of the ocean,
so must I never live
my life for itself,
but always in
the experience which is
going on around me.
It is an uncomfortable
doctrine which the true
ethics whisper into my ear.
You are happy, they say;
therefore you
are called upon
to give much.*

ALBERT SCHWEITZER

You have not
done enough,
you have never
done enough,
so long as it is still
possible that you have
something to contribute.

DAG HAMMARSKJÖLD

How Much Is Enough?

If you see service as a painful duty, then Dag Hammarskjöld's quote on the facing page must read like a sentence of doom.

If, however, you believe that service is bliss, then Mr. Hammarskjöld's comment is a joyful thought: we will have the opportunity to give right up until the end. (And who knows whether the end is not just another beginning?)

Even at the end, we can serve others *by allowing them to serve us.*

More about this as we get toward the end of this book. Now, we are only at the end of part one.

*Life is mostly froth
and bubble,
Two things stand
like stone,
Kindness in
another's trouble,
Courage in your own.*

ADAM LINDSAY GORDON

Ye Wearie Wayfarer

1833–1870

Part Two

We Give to Ourselves

*Everything has
a crack in it—
that's how
the light gets in.*

LEONARD COHEN

Light

Light is a concept that permeates all religions, most philosophies, and several sciences (quantum physics is based upon it). Stated simply, light is the energy that permeates all things.

This light responds to human thought.

One of the greatest gifts we can give is to "send the light."

We send light—either to ourselves or to others—by saying (or thinking), "I ask the light to be sent to_____for their highest good and the highest good of all concerned." That's it; that's sending the light.

We add "for the highest good of all concerned" to keep our personal wants and desires (what *we* think best) out of the situation. (As inconceivable as it may seem, we may not *always* know what's best for *all* people in *all* situations.) We send the light "for the highest good of all concerned" so that *just in case* our thoughts on how something should be *just happen* to be *slightly* inaccurate, the highest good will nonetheless take place.

Sending light for the highest good of all concerned allows us to relax. We can trust that whatever happens after sending the light for the highest good of all concerned *is* for the highest good of all concerned. We need not feverishly manipulate the outcome to be whatever *we* think best.

More light!

GOETHE'S LAST WORDS

Sending the light—to yourself, to another, or to a situation—can be done anywhere, anytime. It takes only a second (literally). The next time you're detained at a traffic light, send the light. The next time you're standing in line, consider it a "send-the-light line." The next time you're put on hold, don't just hold your temper; send the light.

Before setting out to physically be of service, we suggest that you ask the light to surround, fill, protect, bless, and heal you for your highest good, the highest good of all you come into contact with, and the highest good of all concerned. This "armor of light" acts both as a shield and as a vehicle through which some of our more profound gifts can be given.

Light lightens the load and lights the path.

Light also encompasses the concept of taking all life—and especially ourselves—a little more lightly. "You grow up the day you have your first real laugh," said Ethel Barrymore, "—at yourself."

If you add some light you'll probably find that if something's going to be funny later (as a great anecdote for your friends in which you *add* bad stuff that never occurred just to make it more entertaining), it's funny as it's happening. The affirmation for these situations: "Relax. This is funny." Or, simply, "Lighten up!"

*To keep a lamp
burning we have to
keep putting oil in it.*

MOTHER TERESA

Keep the Home Fires Burning

Naturally, before we can be of service to others, we must be of service to ourselves. If we don't, eventually someone will have to be of service to us.

The obvious example is someone who is so busy giving, giving, giving to others that he or she takes no time for rest, food, or even water. How long will this person hold up?

One who takes time for "selfish" acts of rest, food, and water—plus a little re-creation—will be of much greater service over a longer period of time than one who "sacrifices everything" for others.

Our first call to service is to give to ourselves—to take care of our basic needs for food, water, shelter, clothing, health. Once our primary needs—and a few fundamental wants—are met, the rest is overflow.

The overflow is to be given away. This is not a "rule"; it is simply what those who are natural givers do. Givers need to give. After the basic needs of life are met, givers enjoy giving more than they enjoy receiving.

What to a taker would be a sacrifice, to a giver is a privilege.

♥ ♥ ♥

In our book, *LIFE 101: Everything We Wish We Had Learned About Life In School—But Didn't,* when we *did* give "rules" (more suggestions, really), they were:

*Wisdom is the power
that enables us to use knowledge
for the benefit of ourselves
and others.*

THOMAS J. WATSON

*If wisdom were offered me
with the proviso that
I should keep it shut up
and refrain from declaring it,
I should refuse.
There's no delight in owning
anything unshared.*

SENECA

First Century

Don't hurt yourself and don't hurt others.

Take care of yourself so you may help take care of others.

Use everything for your upliftment, learning, and growth.

All we're saying in this chapter is an elaboration of "Take care of yourself so you may help take care of others." No one *has* to take care of others, but those who choose to, want to, or need to, *may* take care of others only by taking care of themselves first.

*If we do more
with less,
our resources will
be adequate
to take care
of everybody.*

BUCKMINSTER FULLER

Taking Care of vs. Indulging Ourselves

Givers want to give. Unfortunately, givers are programmed by our society to "be like everyone else"—that is, to *get*.

Yes, our society pays a certain amount of lip service to giving, but most of our cultural messages involve the joys, satisfactions, and importance of obtaining, consuming, getting more. If we had a national cheer, it would probably be "More! More! More!"

The United States has 5% of the world's population yet consumes approximately 70% of the world's resources. (We also produce an inordinate amount of the world's pollution.)

Let's face it: we are a nation of gluttons—and we are trained to believe this gluttony is *good*.

Some say we should just raise the standard of living for everyone on the planet to that of our own. Nice dream for, oh, 1953. We now know—at least with our current technology—that is impossible. For every family in China to own a refrigerator, for example, the escaping Freon just to manufacture them would completely destroy the ozone, and there goes the earth. And that's just refrigerators for China! The American Dream, infinitely exported, would be a global nightmare. (To a certain degree, in fact, it already is.)

*If my hands are fully
occupied in holding
on to something,
I can neither give
nor receive.*

DOROTHEE SÖLLE

Some givers say, "I'll make more; then I'll give of the overflow." Some "givers" have been saying this for years. Some "givers" have made more, and rather than giving, they fell into the cultural trap of *glamour.*

The overflow that was *supposed* to be used for giving was used to fill their swimming pools.

Perhaps the answer is to live more simply and give of the overflow *we already have.* This will make you a giver—and the Universe tends to give to *true* givers.

We are rich
only through
what we give,
and poor
only through
what we refuse.

ANNE-SOPHIE SWETCHINE

1869

Learn to Receive

True givers receive in strange ways. By "true givers," we mean people who are *actually, physically involved in an ongoing process of giving;* people who are not just *committed* to giving, but people who actually *give.*

True givers know that they are merely caretakers—nothing more than warehousers and distributors of life's stuff. Stuff comes in; they find a need for it; stuff goes out. Stuff in; stuff out.

When the Universe (God, Mother Nature, the Tooth Fairy—whomever or whatever you see as the benevolent, giving force) wants to give to those who need, to whom do you suppose the Universe chooses to distribute these gifts? The givers, of course: the *true* givers.

So, if you're a true giver, learn to receive.

Things will come in the most amazing, unexpected ways. Don't evaluate whether *you* need them or not; receive them with gratitude on behalf of those you will eventually give them to (or, more accurately, pass them along to).

"Blessed are those who can give without remembering," wrote Elizabeth Bibesco, "and take without forgetting."

Receiving is one of the most difficult things for givers to do. The key is: *don't take it personally.* Even if it is something you can use and will use for yourself, accept it in the spirit that, "This is one less thing I will have to supply for

*The art of acceptance
is the art of making
someone who has just
done you a small favor
wish that he might
have done you
a greater one.*

RUSSELL LYNES

myself, so I will have more time and energy to supply the needs of others."

True givers often make their living by giving.

Many say, "I'd like a job like that!" Give—*truly* give—and a job giving to others will eventually be given to you. Don't pursue the job; pursue the service, and the job will pursue you.

Why do you look at
the speck of sawdust
in your brother's eye
and pay no attention
to the plank
in your own eye?
How can you say
to your brother,
"Brother, let me take the
speck out of your eye,"
when you yourself fail
to see the plank
in your own eye?
You hypocrite,
first take the plank out
of your eye, and then
you will see clearly
to remove the speck
from your brother's eye.

JESUS OF NAZARETH
Luke 6:41–42

Server, Heal Thyself

Whenever we have the desire to "fix" or change someone in the name of service, perhaps it's good to remember the proverb, "Physician, heal yourself!"*

It's fine to serve, of course—to nurture, to care for, to support, even to offer good advice—*when asked* or when another is *clearly open* to it.

When, however, we feel an overwhelming need to give another an invaluable flake of our wisdom which they seem completely disinterested in hearing—much less following—then perhaps it's time to heal ourselves.

What if that person is serving *us* by holding up a mirror and reflecting back to us one of our own weaknesses?

That golden nugget of wisdom he or she so foolishly disregarded need not go to waste—it can be used after all: *on us*. We can find some way to apply that sage advice to ourselves. And apply it.

There's no need to be perfect before we start giving—there are plenty of people who are *right now* waiting for what we have to give, in the way we already know how to give it. In order to help more people at a higher level, how-

*Two thousand years ago, it was already a proverb. Jesus said, "Surely you will quote this proverb to me: 'Physician, heal yourself!'" (Luke 4:23)

*There is no human
problem which could
not be solved if people
would simply do
as I advise.*

GORE VIDAL

ever, we must grow to a higher level ourselves.

And what's one of the best ways for givers to grow?

*If you want to lift
yourself up,
lift up someone else.*

BOOKER T. WASHINGTON

Servers, Heal Thyselves— Through Service, Of Course

It's the old wisdom: "How do I get my hand clean?" "By washing your other hand." Or, as the saying said, "You can't help someone uphill without getting closer to the top yourself."

Whether we want to grow to new and dynamic levels of experience and expression, or whether we want to keep ourselves from going insane, service can be a valuable vehicle.*

The noted psychiatrist Karl Menninger was asked what he would recommend if someone felt a nervous breakdown coming on. "Lock up your house," he advised, "go across the railroad tracks, and find someone in need and do something for him."

Our physical health may depend upon giving as well. "The house which is not opened for charity," says the Talmud, "will be opened to the physician." In study after study, those who regularly give are healthier, happier, and live longer than those primarily involved in getting.

If you're one of those people who live to give, then give to live.

---

*If you *really* think you are going insane, by all means check with a health care professional *at once*. Remember to take care of yourself first. The "insane" that we're talking about here are the run-of-the-mill "crazies" we all have from time to time.

It is one of the
beautiful compensations
of this life
that no one can
sincerely try
to help another
without helping himself.

CHARLES DUDLEY WARNER

*When you find yourself
overpowered, as it were,
by melancholy,
the best way
is to go out
and do something kind
to somebody or other.*

JOHN KEBLE

1792–1866

*There is nothing
to make you like
other human beings
so much as doing
things for them.*

ZORA NEALE HURSTON

We Give Not to Be Liked, But to Like

Sometimes we have trouble liking others—loving is no problem; it's *liking* that's tough.

"I love humanity," someone once observed, "it's *people* I can't stand."

For givers, the best way to like someone is to do something for them. We know this goes against conventional wisdom, but givers, as you may have noticed, find wisdom in unconventional ways.

*We are better pleased
to see those on whom
we confer benefits
than those from whom
we receive them.*

LA ROCHEFOUCAULD

1665

*Men become attached
to us not by reason
of the services
we render them,
but by reason
of the services
they render us.*

EUGÈNE LABICHE

1860

Knowing sorrow well,
I learn the way to
succor the distressed.

VERGIL

19 B.C.

Givers Find, Even in Pain, An Additional Compensation

Walking through the many dark valleys in this life—pain, sorrow, loss, hurt, anger, worry, frustration, illness, and the rest—all people gain value by (a) surviving them (b) overcoming them, and (one hopes) (c) learning something from them.

Givers, however, have an additional compensation: *they can use the experience and what they've learned to be of greater service to others.*

We become more compassionate. We can say to someone, "I've been there," and the other person will know we speak the truth.

We are more understanding. Where the less experienced might say, "Oh, just snap out of it," we might know that "snapping out of it" is not an option for this person at this time.

We are more able to *be* with a person, to let the person know he or she is not alone, to help the person believe that healing lies ahead. We might even be able to offer suggestions—based on our own experience—that can speed the healing along.

Sometimes, something "bad" happens to us and we ask, "Why did this happen?" It doesn't seem to apply to our lives at all—whatever lessons might be gained don't seem to be directly applicable to our lives. Then, weeks, months, sometimes years later, someone will come along

Full of love
for all things
in the world,
practicing virtue
in order
to benefit others,
this man alone
is happy.

BUDDHA

with *precisely* that problem and we not only understand it, we also have compassion for it—and, often, a solution. At those points we realize we didn't go through the experience for *us;* we went through the experience for *the other person.* (Of course, we *did* go through it for us, because we asked for opportunities to give, and this was just one of them, or the preparation—the *training*—for one of them.)

So, "when you find yourself in times of trouble," as the Beatles sang, ask not only, "How can I help myself out of this," but also, "How can I use this to help others?"

Service school is in session.

The man who lives
for himself is a failure.
Even if he gains
much wealth, position or power
he still is a failure.
The man who lives for others
has achieved true success.
A rich man who consecrates
his wealth and his position
to the good of humanity
is a success.
A poor man who
gives of his service
and his sympathy to others
has achieved true success
even though material prosperity
or outward honors
never come to him.

NORMAN VINCENT PEALE

When We Give to Something Greater Than Ourselves, We Become Greater, Too

When we give to someone, something, or some cause greater than ourselves, we feel transcendent and expanded. The person, thing, or cause we give to becomes greater for our gift, and—seemingly violating the law of physics—we become greater too.

This happens because giving does not follow the law of physics; giving follows the law of service. In service, all good is multiplied. Jesus demonstrated this with the multiplication of the loaves and the fishes:

> By this time it was late in the day, so his disciples came to him. "This is a remote place," they said, "and it's already very late. Send the people away so they can go to the surrounding countryside and villages and buy themselves something to eat."
>
> But he answered, "You give them something to eat."
>
> They said to him, "That would take eight months of a man's wages! Are we to go and spend that much on bread and give it to them to eat?"
>
> "How many loaves do you have?" he asked. "Go and see."
>
> When they found out, they said, "Five—and two fish."
>
> Then Jesus directed them to have all the

The sage does not
accumulate for himself.
The more he uses
for others,
the more he has
himself.
The more he
gives to others,
the more he possesses
of his own.
The Way of Heaven is
to benefit others
and not to injure.

LAO-TZU

c. 604–531 B.C.

people sit down in groups on the green grass. So they sat down in groups of hundreds and fifties.

Taking the five loaves and the two fish and looking up to heaven, he gave thanks and broke the loaves. Then he gave them to his disciples to set before the people. He also divided the two fish among them all.

They all ate and were satisfied, and the disciples picked up twelve basketfuls of broken pieces of bread and fish. The number of the men who had eaten was five thousand. (Mark 6:35–44)

Adding our gift to something greater than ourselves multiplies the good for all.

The giving of money,
time, support,
and encouragement
to worthy causes can
never be detrimental
to the giver.
The laws of nature
are structured so that
acts of charity
will open an individual
to an unbounded
reservoir of riches.

JEFFREY MOSES

Condemned to Give

While we are alive, our service never stops. We are doomed to be of service. If you do nothing else, every time you exhale, you are being of service to the entire plant kingdom.

Animals take in oxygen and give off carbon dioxide. Plants take in carbon dioxide and give off oxygen. This mutual giving and receiving between the plant and animal kingdoms is one of the primary attributes of *life*.

We give because not to give means death. Each time we exhale, we give carbon dioxide to plants: whichever plant gets it first, uses it. We may never receive anything directly from that plant; in fact, we don't even get to know which plant received it.

If, for some reason, however, you wanted to *withhold* your carbon dioxide from plants (perhaps you agree with the person who said, "I'm not a vegetarian because I love animals; I'm a vegetarian because I hate plants") and hold your breath, soon it would hurt so much you'd give in and give. Even if you could withstand the pain, eventually you'd pass out. *Then* the plants would get your gift.

It's hopeless.

We are condemned to give.

*If things are not
going well with you,
begin your effort at
correcting the
situation by carefully
examining the service
you are rendering,
and especially the
spirit
in which you are
rendering it.*

ROGER BABSON

Give Quiz

Which are the magic words that transform a heartless exchange into heartfelt service?

a) Alacazam

b) Attitude

c) Abracadabra

d) Altitude

Answer: Attitude and Altitude. (If the other ones work, by all means use them—"Whatever works" is our slogan.)

Let's take a closer look at attitude and altitude.

*If you're not fired
with enthusiasm,
you will be fired
with enthusiasm.*

VINCE LOMBARDI

Attitude

Let's explore a fairly typical entry-level work situation: bagging burgers at the back of the local burger emporium. You may not see the people you serve. You may not even know how many people you serve: for every hundred burgers you wrap, you may have fed a hundred schoolchildren or two very hungry tourists. This is the type of work that can be a job or a joy depending upon your *(ta da!)* attitude.

The extremes in attitude the burger wrapper (the person, not the paper) could take:

"I'm so pleased I can help provide nourishment for my fellow human beings and do the best possible job I can for my boss."

Or:

"Damn wrappers, damn customers, damn burgers, damn boss, damn job, damn life."

Somewhere between *Pollyanna in Burgerland* and *The Burgerwrappers of the Damned* lies the range of attitudes that can make precisely the same activity either heartfelt service or heart-burdening servitude.

From the purely practical point of view, Milan R. Bump cautions:

> If your work is work to you and you don't see beyond that work and see the pleasure in work and the pleasure in service, look out; you are in danger of standing in your present station for a long, long time.

*"I have got to take
a few pints of soup
to the deserving poor,"
said Myrtle.
"I'd better set about it.
Amazing the way
these bimbos
absorb soup.
Like sponges."*

P. G. WODEHOUSE

Wrapping burgers with the conscious knowledge that you are making a *contribution* opens the heart. Counting the hours and cursing each burger closes the heart. It's a matter of attitude, and attitude is a matter of choice.

It certainly may not *seem* as though attitude is a matter of choice: our reactions seem so automatic. Our conditioning and our body-born conditions (genetics) make it appear that life is either a rose bush with thorns or a thorn bush with roses. Whether we focus on roses or thorns, however, is a choice.

With practice, we can recognize the programming earlier and earlier and challenge its seemingly inevitable results. (For more information on this, please read our book, *You Can't Afford the Luxury of a Negative Thought.)*

In time, a burger wrapper can watch the order for an extra hundred burgers come in and make a conscious choice: "Do I wrap these burgers with the attitude of heartfelt service or do I wrap these burgers with the attitude of heart-burdening servitude?" The choice will always be respected.

Eventually, we can reprogram ourselves to automatically see each request of our time, energy, or talents as an opportunity to serve. We may not be able to honor all requests, but those we do will be done with a loving heart.

From a distance
the earth looks
blue and green
and the snow-capped
mountains white.
From a distance
the ocean meets
the stream
and the eagle
takes to flight.
From a distance
there is harmony
and it echoes
through the land.
It's the voice of hope.
It's the voice of peace.
It's the voice of every man.

JULIE GOLD

Altitude

In the 1960s, there was a Rocky and Bullwinkle cartoon in which Bullwinkle Moose launches Rocky, the flying squirrel, into the air. Rocky, soaring at cloud-level, looks down on the situation that formerly seemed perplexing.

"I see it all now!" exclaims Rocky.

"Well, you should, Rock," says Bullwinkle, "you're high enough."

That's what altitude does for us: it puts everything in perspective. As the Rocky part of us soars above and "sees it all now," the Bullwinkle part of us remains earth-bound, walking through life.

When we get "above it all" through meditation, contemplation, inspiration (reading, listening to tapes and lectures, taking workshops, counseling), or other uplifting activities, we can see that life is nothing *but* service.

serving us so that we might serve others

*For every action
there is an equal
and opposite reaction.
If you want
to receive a great deal,
you first have to give
a great deal.
If each individual
will give of himself
to whomever he can,
wherever he can,
in any way that he can,
in the long run he will be
compensated in the exact
proportion that he gives.*

R. A. HAYWARD

We Give to Get

The Hindus and most Eastern religions call it karma: what you do comes back to you.

The Jewish scriptures proclaim: "Cast thy bread upon the waters: for thou shalt find it after many days" (Ecclesiastes 11:1).

The Christian version was stated by Paul: "For whatsoever a man soweth, that shall he also reap" (Galatians 6:7*). "Let us not become weary in doing good, for at the proper time we will reap a harvest if we do not give up" (Galatians 6:9**).

In the 'hood, the same idea is simply stated, "What goes around, comes around."

This idea is such a universal and timeless one, that we would venture to put it into the category of "Truth." ("That's Truth spelled with a great big T," Joan Baez sang, "and peddled in the mystic's booth.")

If "what you sow you reap" is an answer, then the next question is: "What kind of harvest would you like?"

---

*That was the King James Version. The New International Version is even more straightforward: "A man reaps what he sows."

**That was the New International Version. The King James Version *might* be more accurate on this point: "And let us not be weary in well doing: for in due season we shall reap, if we faint not."

*The person who sows
seeds of kindness
enjoys a perpetual
harvest.*

*One of the most
difficult things to give
away is kindness;
it usually comes
back to you.*

It's what each of us sows,
and how, that gives to us
character and prestige.
Seeds of kindness, goodwill,
and human understanding,
planted in fertile soil,
spring up
into deathless friendships,
big deeds of worth,
and a memory that
will not soon fade out.
We are all sowers
of seeds—
and let us never forget it!

GEORGE MATTHEW ADAMS

The Takers May Eat Better, But the Givers Sleep Better

What we give returns to us. What we give, then, determines the currents and the currency of our lives.

What do you want most? Loving? Compassion? Caring? Tenderness? Laughter? Joy? Money? Whatever it is (or they are), give it away. Like Sting's message in a bottle, what you give out will return to you.

At that point, you can choose to spend it, (use it, enjoy it, feel it, and so on), or you can give it away again. (Certainly, you can enjoy it while it passes through your hands—or heart.) Given away, it returns again—and usually faster than the first time. Give it away again, and it returns again. Give, return. Give-return.

Soon it's hard to tell whether all that loving, compassion, caring, tenderness, laughing, joy, and money is coming or going.

Eventually, it's not a matter of giving and then receiving (for example) love (currency), but becomes a steady *flow* of loving (current)— a *consciousness* of loving.

*They who give
have all things;
they who withhold
have nothing.*

HINDU PROVERB

*There is an ordinary
proverb for this:
"Stinginess
does not enrich;
charity does not
impoverish."*

GLÜCKEL OF HAMELN

1719

Our deeds determine us,
as much as we
determine our deeds.

GEORGE ELIOT

Service Is Becoming

Ultimately, it's not a matter of what we *receive* from giving, but what we *become* by giving that matters.

"The profit on a good action is to have done it," wrote Seneca 1900-or-so years ago. To paraphrase Seneca's thought: "The profit on a good action is to become it."

*For it is in giving
that we receive.*

FRANCIS OF ASSISI

c. 1181–1226

Giving Is Such a Selfish Thing (Sneak Preview)

As we end this section on giving to ourselves, allow us to mention again that the primary benefit givers get from giving is the joy of giving itself.

Giving is such a selfish thing. (Now where have we heard *that* before?)

Part eight of this book explores the delightful paradox that the more givers give, the more selfish they're being.

But first, let's discuss some acts of *seeming* unselfishness.

*Come,
give us a taste
of your quality.*

SHAKESPEARE

Part Three

We Give to Others

*It is
hideous and coarse
to assume that
we can do
something
for others—
and it is
vile
not to endeavor
to do it.*

EDWARD DAHLBERG

The Dilemmas of Giving to Others

Giving to others has certain built-in problems. It seems to bring out the best—and the worst—in people.

We would be remiss (that is, not serving you, the reader) if we focused on only the "feel good" of what is called by some charity and philanthropy, and called by others meddling and do-gooding.

In giving to others, here are just a few of the dilemmas:

- How can we possibly know what another *truly* needs, how can we presume to think that we have what it takes to fill that need, and how can we possibly not try?

- In giving to others, are we supporting them or supporting their weaknesses?

- Does this situation need the caring of an amateur, or the skill of a professional?

- How do we know whether we're helping or interfering, putting an end to pain or cutting short a necessary process, supporting or meddling?

- How can we tell if we're being courageous or merely stupid?

All of this on top of our own *personal* fear,

*The spirit in which
a thing is given
determines that
in which the debt
is acknowledged;
it's the intention,
not the face-value
of the gift,
that's weighed.*

SENECA

First Century

guilt, hurt feelings, anger, and unworthiness (a.k.a. the comfort zone) that naturally arise in any new situation.

We'll explore these points as we go along. We do not plan to offer pat answers: your answers are already inside of you. We do plan to offer enough questions, techniques, and *possible* answers—from many points of view—for you to discover *your* answers.

For now, three suggestions to ponder:

1. When giving to others, use your heart *and* your head.

2. To the degree you can, don't confuse your *emotions* with your *intuition*.

3. When it comes to your physical safety or the physical safety of another—when in doubt, don't.

We certainly don't mean to *add* to your fear with these suggestions. It's just that some people feel "the spirit of giving" and drive alone to the worst part of town at two o'clock in the morning and begin handing out flowers. Not a good idea. Handing out flowers in the park at two in the afternoon or volunteering for an organization that regularly hands out flour in the ghetto is a better idea.

Simply: don't leave your common sense at home when you go out to serve.

*Give light
and the people
will find
their own way.*

MOTTO OF THE

SCRIPPS-HOWARD

NEWSPAPERS

What Do We Give?

What have you got? Talent? Kindness? Love? Patience? Are you a good listener? Can you cook? Paint? Balance books? Make little horses out of pipe cleaners? Sing? Clean toilets? Do you happen to know the president's (*any* president's) private phone number? Does he or she owe you a favor? Do you know how to play "Chopsticks"? Use chopsticks? Make chopsticks? Do you have the use of a car? Storefront? Lecture hall? Barn? Warehouse? Forty acres in the great white North? A bicycle? Are you good at making silly lists? Let's end *this* silly list with that mainstay of service: *money*.

Whatever you've got, it can be a gift to others—even the seeming negatives. What's, uh, manure to you is organic fertilizer to the farmer.

A member of Dr. Carlo DiGiovanna's congregation who complained about *everything* also volunteered for everything. The volunteering was appreciated, but the complaining was driving everyone nuts. Eventually, he discovered the place to use his complaining volunteer best: he put the congregate in charge of complaining *for* the church. Any difficulty with the city, suppliers, repair people, or any other professional disputes were turned over to the one-person Bureau of Dispute Resolution. It worked brilliantly.

A part of giving is finding a useful recipient of the gift.

*The first great gift
we can bestow on others
is a good example.*

THOMAS MORELL

Give what you have.
To someone,
it may be better
than you
dare to think.

LONGFELLOW

Anticipate charity
by preventing poverty;
assist the reduced
fellowman,
either by
a considerable gift,
or a sum of money,
or by teaching him a
trade, or by putting him
in the way of business,
so that he may earn
an honest livelihood,
and not be forced
to the dreadful alternative
of holding out his hand
for charity.
This is the highest step
and the summit
of charity's golden ladder.

MAIMONIDES
Twelfth-Century Jewish Sage

The Eight Grades of Charity:

1. *to give reluctantly*
2. *to give cheerfully but not adequately*
3. *to give cheerfully and adequately,
   but only after being asked*
4. *to give cheerfully, adequately,
   and of your own free will,
   but to put it in the recipient's hand
   in such a way as to make him feel lesser*
5. *to let the recipient know who
   the donor is, but not the reverse*
6. *to know who is receiving your charity
   but to remain anonymous to him*
7. *to have neither the donor nor the
   recipient be aware of the other's identity*
8. *to dispense with charity altogether,
   by enabling your fellow humans
   to have the wherewithal
   to earn their own living.*

MAIMONIDES

Don't be selfish.
If you have something
you do not want,
and know someone
who has no use for it,
give.
In this way
you can be generous
without expenditure
of self-denial and
also help another
to be the same.

ELBERT HUBBARD

*Philanthropy is the
refuge of people who
wish to annoy
their fellow creatures.*

OSCAR WILDE

*We often excuse
our own want
of philanthropy
by giving the name
of fanaticism to the
more ardent zeal
of others.*

LONGFELLOW

*For those who
are not hungry,
it is easy to palaver
about the degradation
of charity.*

CHARLOTTE BRONTË

1849

*Avarice hoards
itself poor;
charity gives
itself rich.*

GERMAN PROVERB

Charity,
as if it didn't
have enough trouble
in this day and age,
will always be suspected
of morbidity—
sado-masochism,
perversity of some sort.
All higher or moral
tendencies lie
under suspicion
of being rackets.
Things we simply honor
with old words,
but betray or deny
in our very nerves.

SAUL BELLOW

*He that gives his heart
will not deny his money.*

THOMAS FULLER, M.D.

1732

Sometimes, the Gift People Appreciate Most Is Something You Made Yourself— Such As Money

Money is simply a *symbol of energy*. We trade a valuable (energy-filled) item, idea, or activity for a symbol of its value (its energy) —money. We then exchange that symbol of energy (money) for another item, idea, or activity that we consider valuable.

Because money represents our energy, it is an extension of ourselves.

Money represents a personal investment on our part—a symbol of our work, energy, ideas, or good fortune. As such, when we give money we *are* giving of ourselves.

"Oh, they only give *money,* they don't give of *themselves,*" some say. People saying this are usually poor. (With that sort of poverty consciousness, it's not surprising.)

Of course, love, affection, tenderness, and simply *being there* are essential to service.

So is money.

Until the time that you can simply announce, "I'm on a service project!" and are immediately given unlimited supplies of food, tools, transportation, office space, printing, telephones, housing, aspirin, and all the other

Money-giving
is a very good criterion
of a person's
mental health.
Generous people
are rarely
mentally ill people.

KARL A. MENNINGER, M.D.

goods and services necessary for service, money will be as important to the act of giving as the love that inspires the act.

*For too many giving is
occasional, spasmodic,
ill-proportioned.
It depends
on what is left over
when other things
have had their full share.
Sometimes
what it means is
that only the small change
lying in their pockets
goes to the support
of good and worthy causes.*

ROBERT J. MCCRACKEN, D.D.

*Riches may enable us
to confer favours,
but to confer them
with propriety and grace
requires a something
that riches cannot give.*

CHARLES CALEB COLTON

*The deed is all,
not the glory.*

GOETHE

There Is No Limit to the Good You Can Do If You Don't Care Who Gets the Credit

People often interpret the term "selfless service" to mean *altruism*—giving to others with absolutely no thought of return. As we have pointed out before (and will point out again), we give because it feels good to give. The recipient is but an innocent bystander.

There is, however, a more useful definition of "selfless service": giving with no thought of credit, reward, or appreciation from the recipient or the world at large.

Part of the fun of giving is doing it anonymously. ("The greatest gift is to fill a need unnoticed.") Like the Lone Ranger, who never waited around to be thanked, leaving the grateful townspeople to ponder, "Who *was* that masked man?" we (the authors) like to do good, disappear, and leave those in our wake wondering, "Who were those two crazy fools?"

The Lone Donor rides again. "Hi-ho service, away!"

Sometimes, of course, making a public display of giving inspires (or shames) others into giving, too. ("What a generous thing to do! I think I'll donate some money, too." "This idiot donated enough money for the new wing of a building. *I'll* donate enough money for a whole building!")

*Noble deeds
are most estimable
when hidden.*

PASCAL

1670

Not everyone who donates publicly, then, is in it for the glory; many organizations find that well-publicized gifts—especially from famous people—encourage gifts from others.

Elizabeth Taylor, for example, who has money, prestige, and power, didn't have to do another thing for her name to be preserved in film history. Nevertheless, she decided in the mid-1980s—long before it became popular or even acceptable—to support research in finding the cure for AIDS and to provide care (and caring) for people with AIDS. She took a risk and, with that risk, put her fame, money, and prestige on the line because she wanted to serve.

Similarly, Mary Tyler Moore, who is among the richest women in show business (according to *Fortune),* still does a great many public appearances, which she would never do for mere money. She is the spokesperson for the Juvenile Diabetes Foundation and, as such, she makes appearances as an expression of her giving.

Barbra Streisand, who has won the highest awards in all fields of entertainment (Oscar, Tony, Emmy, Grammy, etc., etc.) also deserves the highest award for service, too. She has given public concerts for political candidates and to support AIDS care and research. (According to her rumored Las Vegas salary, these appearances are worth ten million dollars each!) She speaks out on fairness, justice, freedom, and decency at every opportunity. She donated her multi-million dollar Malibu estate to a land conservation organization. (The highest award for service, by the way, is not a plaque, certificate, or statuette: it is given to and proudly warms the heart of the giver.)

*So when you give
to the needy,
do not announce it
with trumpets,
as the hypocrites do
in the synagogues
and on the streets,
to be honored by men.
I tell you the truth,
they have received
their reward in full.
But when you give
to the needy, do not let
your left hand know
what your right hand
is doing, so that your
giving may be in secret.
Then your Father,
who sees what is done
in secret, will reward you.*

JESUS OF NAZARETH
Matthew 6:2–4

*It is with
narrow-souled people
as with narrow-necked
bottles: the less they
have in them
the more noise they make
in pouring it out.*

ALEXANDER POPE

*Don't use the
impudence of a beggar
as an excuse
for not helping him.*

RABBI SCHMELKE
OF NICOLSBURG

Be Kind to Unkind People— They May Need It Most

Some people spend an inordinate amount of time and energy making sure that the recipients of their gifts are *truly* deserving and have the right *attitude*.

Frankly, if they had the right attitude, they probably wouldn't need your gift.

*Kindness is loving people
more than they deserve.*

JOSEPH JOUBERT

Isn't it better to have men being ungrateful than to miss a chance to do good?

DENIS DIDEROT

The highest exercise
of charity is
charity towards
the uncharitable.

J. S. BUCKMINSTER

He that returns
a good for evil
obtains the victory.

THOMAS FULLER, M.D.

*Kind looks,
kind words, kind acts,
and warm handshakes—
these are secondary
means of grace when
men are in trouble
and are fighting
their unseen battles.*

JOHN HALL

Another Reason for Giving

In addition to the ones already given, certainly one of the reasons givers "wish to scatter joy and not pain around us," as Emerson put it, is because there is already entirely too much pain in the world.

This is not an easy life.

Those with feelings can feel the pain in their own lives; those with compassion can feel the pain in others'. Those who feel this pain, this darkness, have no desire to add to the darkness.

Givers intuitively want to ease burdens, lighten loads, spread light.

Let no one
underestimate
the need of pity.
We live in a stony
universe whose hard,
brilliant forces
rage fiercely.

THEODORE DREISER

*Kindness is
gladdening the hearts
of those who are
traveling the dark
journey with us.*

HENRI-FRÉDÉRIC AMIEL

*Let us not paralyze
our capacity for good
by brooding over man's
capacity for evil.*

DAVID SARNOFF

Don't Let Darkness Darken Your Spirit

Givers, being compassionate, are often more aware of the pain in this world than others. Most people who create the pain, in fact, are quite unaware that they are doing so. *Unconscious* seems to be the term that best describes these people. They are "the little foxes, that spoil the vines: for our vines have tender grapes" (Song of Songs 2:15).

The challenge for givers, in a world that seems bent on destruction and pain, is how to keep giving anyway.

It is worth the effort. A single candle can overcome a lot of darkness.

As Henry James put it:

> We work in the dark—we do what we can—we give what we have. Our doubt is our passion, and our passion is our task. The rest is the madness of art.

*It is better to light
a candle than to
curse the darkness.*

CHINESE PROVERB

Adopted as the motto of the Christophers

*How far that little
candle throws
his beams!
So shines a good deed
in a naughty world.*

SHAKESPEARE

*It hurteth not
the tongue to give
fair words.*

JOHN HEYWOOD

1546

Speak Kind Words

What we say, and the way in which we say it, can be an important part of giving. Our choice of words and our tone of voice can calm, excite, soothe, or inspire.

As Proverbs (16:23) points out, "A wise man's heart guides his mouth."

Even criticism can be given in a positive way. A friend of ours, an actress famous for her physical allure, sometimes walks up to a strange man, whispers in his ear, "You're far too sexy to smoke," smiles, and continues on her way. If we smoked, we would find this a far greater incentive to quit than someone lecturing us, "Don't you know how *bad* smoking is for you?!"

Sometimes uplifting words left on answering machines or notes of support written on a postcard (discreetly worded, of course—it is, after all, a postcard) take only a minute or two of our time but can provide hours or even days of encouragement to others.

Words are powerful. You are powerful. Giving is powerful. Imagine how powerfully helpful it can be when these three combine.

Kind words do not
cost much.
They never blister the
tongue or lips.
Mental trouble was never
known to arise
from such quarters.
Though they do not
cost much yet they
accomplish much.
They make other people
good natured.
They also produce their
own image on men's souls,
and a beautiful image it is.

PASCAL

*The most difficult
part is to give.
Then why not
add a smile?*

JEAN DE LA BRUYÈRE

1645–1696

Keep the other person's well-being in mind when you feel an attack of soul-purging truth coming on.

BETTY WHITE

If you can't be kind,
at least be vague.

MISS MANNERS

The love of our neighbor
in all its fullness
simply means being
able to say to him,
"What are you
going through?"

SIMONE WEIL

Listen

Sometimes the greatest gift is not saying a word. Ten minutes of active, compassionate, nonjudgmental listening can often do more than several hours of dispensing "good advice."

When others know that talking to us is a "safe space" in which they can say anything they want without thought of reprisal, condemnation, or fear of having a confidence betrayed, they not only find comfort in being able to speak about their difficulty, but often find their own solutions as well.

Earlier, we quoted the Scripps-Howard newspapers' motto, "Give light and the people will find their own way."

We might modify that slightly to read, "Give light, lend a compassionate ear, and the people will find their own way."

In the sick room,
ten cents' worth
of human understanding
equals
ten dollars' worth
of medical science.

MARTIN H. FISCHER

The Gift of Healing

Some know they have the gift of healing; some are not so sure; others deny it. Allow us to make a rather rash generalization, based on decades of watching givers giving:

If you're a true giver, if you put your body on the line in the name of giving, you are a healer.

By taking your compassion, warmth, light, and love to those who need physical, emotional, mental, or spiritual healing, you help healing to take place.

Oh, your visit (or call or card or sending the light) may not bring about an instantaneous complete healing, but a lot more healing happened because you directed your time and intention toward healing.

There is no need to concern yourself with the "hows" of healing—just go give. Healing will happen.

*Pleasant words
are a honeycomb,
sweet to the soul and
healing to the bones.*

PROVERBS 16:24

Happiness, grief,
gaiety, sadness,
are by nature contagious.
Bring your health and
your strength to the
weak and sickly,
and so you will be
of use to them.
Give them,
not your weakness,
but your energy,
so you will revive
and lift them up.
Life alone can
rekindle life.

HENRI-FRÉDÉRIC AMIEL

*I know what
I have given you.
I do not know what
you have received.*

ANTONIO PORCHIA

You Give What You Give; They Get What They Get

Our giving can only go so far. At a certain point, it is up to the other person to receive. When we've given what we can, in the best way we know how, with our best intentions in tow, we can only release the gift with the thought, "for the highest good of all concerned," and let it go.

From that point on, how the gift is received, *what* gift is received—or even if the gift is received at all—is in the hands of another.

"But you cannot give to people what they are incapable of receiving," Agatha Christie observed. An earthier way of saying this comes from Zorba the Greek: "You can knock on the door of the deaf forever."

If it seems as though your service is not—how do we put this delicately?—*appreciated,* take your giving elsewhere.

As givers, of course, it's not appreciation we seek; but if absolutely *no* appreciation is forthcoming, perhaps our gifts would do more good if given elsewhere.

*Do not do unto others
as you would that they
should do unto you.
Their tastes may not
be the same.*

GEORGE BERNARD SHAW

Keep It Golden

When Jesus laid down what is generally known as the golden rule when he said, "Do to others as you would have them do to you" (Luke 6:31*), it was already ancient wisdom. More than five centuries earlier, Confucius had said, "What you do not want done to yourself, do not do to others."

This ancient wisdom is often misinterpreted as, "The things I specifically like having done to me, I should do to others." Or, put more plainly, "What's good for *me* must be good for *everybody*—whether they like it or not."

Frankly, this is the sort of thinking that tarnishes the golden rule.

Just as we want to be done to in ways that we can enjoy, accept, and value, so, too, we must give to others in ways that *they* can enjoy, accept, and value.

If you're going to play "holier than thou," you may end up feeling holy (as in self-righteous), but not being terribly helpful.

Certainly, there's no need to compromise your *principles;* it's just that sometimes, when giving, we must set aside our *preferences.*

---

*Or the slight variation in Matthew 7:12, "So in everything, do to others what you would have them do to you."

All the beautiful
sentiments
in the world
weigh less
than a single
lovely action.

JAMES RUSSELL LOWELL

Do It!*

When it actually comes time to serve, we will be met by the limitations of the comfort zone. The comfort zone is all the activities we have done often enough that we feel comfortable doing them. When serving in a new area, in a new way, or with new people, we often feel uncomfortable. The feelings of discomfort are generally the emotions of fear, guilt, unworthiness, hurt feelings, and anger.

We must be prepared to feel these feelings, and *physically move into service anyway.*

As we move into service,

- fear can become enthusiasm;
- guilt can become the energy to make changes within ourselves;
- unworthiness can remind us that while we are not worthy of everything, we are worthy of service;
- hurt feelings can remind us of how much we care (beneath all hurt feelings is caring); and
- anger, properly modulated, can become

*DO IT! is also the title of a book that—if we hadn't written it, and we weren't so humble—we would endlessly praise and recommend with superlatives that we normally reserve for ice cream. As it is, we can only, in passing, mention we wrote a book entitled, DO IT! Let's Get Off Our Buts and subtly suggest that, have you the time or inclination, you might receive some value in reading it.

I expect to pass
through life but once.
If, therefore,
there be any kindness
I can show,
or any good thing
I can do to any
fellow being,
let me do it now,
and not defer
or neglect it,
as I shall not pass
this way again.

WILLIAM PENN

the energy to make change in the outer world.

Don't wait until you are perfect; don't wait for the perfect opportunity; don't wait for more to give; don't wait for a more deserving recipient; don't wait until you're more comfortable; *don't wait*.

Do it!

Follow your desire
as long as you live;
do not lessen the time
of following desire,
for the wasting of time
is an abomination
to the spirit.

PTAHHOTPE

2350 B.C.

*It is no profit
to have learned well,
if you neglect
to do well.*

PUBLILIUS SYRUS

First Century B.C.

*Men are all alike
in their promises.
It is only in their deeds
that they differ.*

MOLIÈRE

1668

The smallest good deed
is better than
the grandest
good intention.

DUGUET

We should give as we
would receive,
cheerfully, quickly,
and without hesitation;
for there is no grace
in a benefit that sticks
to the fingers.

SENECA

Do It **<u>NOW!</u>**

If you have read this far in the book without taking our earliest advice—to put the book down often and go give—please put the book down *now* and go give.

If you're *still* reading and not doing, allow us to remind you of the story of the terribly timid giver who desperately wanted to do good for others, but could never quite bring herself to do so. Somehow, she always allowed her fear to be greater than her need to give. One day, however, she saw an unfortunate man standing on a street corner, and, moved by compassion, she summoned all her courage, scribbled "Best of luck" on a $100 bill and thrust it into the man's hand as she quickly passed by.

The next day, the man approached the woman, handed her $1,000, and said, "Nice work, lady. Best of Luck paid ten to one."

So, right now, before turning to the next section, *please*—even if it's just a phone call or a postcard—*go give*.

Best of luck!

*Let him that desires
to see others happy,
make haste to give
while his gift
can be enjoyed,
and remember that
every moment of delay
takes away something
from the value
of his benefaction.*

SAMUEL JOHNSON

*You cannot do
a kindness too soon,
for you never know
how soon it will be
too late.*

EMERSON

*He who waits
to do a great deal
of good at once,
will never do anything.*

SAMUEL JOHNSON

*All worthwhile men
have good thoughts,
good ideas and good
intentions—
but precious few of them
ever translate those
into action.*

JOHN HANCOCK FIELD

I tell you the truth,
whatever you did
for one of the least
of these brothers
of mine,
you did for me.

JESUS OF NAZARETH

Matthew 25:40

Part Four

We Give to Family

We are always too busy
for our children;
we never give them
the time or interest
they deserve.
We lavish gifts
upon them;
but the most
precious gift—
our personal association,
which means
so much to them—
we give grudgingly.

MARK TWAIN

Who Is Our Family?

It's unfortunate that the term *family* should be the subject of controversy. The way we define family tends to put us in one camp or another. Is family only our blood relatives, as those who proclaim "family values" seem to believe? Or is family anyone we relate to, love, and nurture in an ongoing way?

In our wishy-washy way (although we like to think of it as sublime diplomacy), we'll answer the question: *Both*.

Our definition of family is anyone (blood relative or not) whom we care about in an ongoing way—often whether we like it or not. As Robert Frost explained:

> Home is the place where,
> When you have to go there,
> They have to take you in.

Put another way, our family are those people we relate to (our *relat*ions), by choice or by chance, through good times and bad.

If this "extended family" view is considered by some "unchristian," we can only quote the following from Mark (3:20–21, 31–35):

> Then Jesus entered a house, and again a crowd gathered, so that he and his disciples were not even able to eat. When his family heard about this, they went to take charge of him, for they said, "He is out of his mind."
>
> Standing outside, they sent someone in to

I teach my child
to look at life
in a thoroughly
materialistic fashion.
If he escapes
and becomes
the sort of person
I hope
he will become,
it will be
because he
sees through the hokum
that I hand out.

E. B. WHITE

call him. A crowd was sitting around him, and they told him, "Your mother and brothers are outside looking for you."

"Who are my mother and my brothers?" he asked. Then he looked at those seated in a circle around him and said, "Here are my mother and my brothers! Whoever does God's will is my brother and sister and mother."

The definition of *family,* then (according to Jesus, anyway), can include people other than blood relatives we choose to call family.

Serve your family well.

*Often we can help
each other most
by leaving each other
alone;
at other times
we need the hand-grasp
and the word of cheer.*

ELBERT HUBBARD

Giving to Blood Relatives

Giving to blood relatives can be some of the easiest, most difficult, most rewarding, most frustrating giving we can do.

Contradictory? Of course. But those who have given to relatives probably know what we mean.

Let's look at all three sides of this family coin.*

---

*Don't forget about a coin's third side: the edge. A lot of our relatives live on the edge—or fear that *we* do. This sometimes makes them edgy. Us, too.

*Perhaps the greatest
social service
that can be
rendered by anybody
to the country
and to mankind
is to bring up a family.*

GEORGE BERNARD SHAW

The Ties That Bind

For some, loving their spouse and raising good children is the highest possible service. Heaven knows, being even *marginally* successful at these goals is service enough for a lifetime.

If you have taken on the monumental task of supporting a spouse and raising a family, you need never look outside the home to be of ongoing, continuous, and one might add, exhaustive (exhausting?) service.

Often good spouses and good parents are the unsung heroes of our time. Allow us, then, to sing their praises:

> La, la, la,
> Hooray for loving spouses
> and nurturing parents
> La, la, la, la, la.

Feel validated, vindicated, acknowledged, and appreciated? We hope so. It might be the most you'll ever get from an outside source. (It might be the most you'll get from an inside source, too.)

As with all service, if you learn to praise yourself once a day for giving well done, you will, at least once each day, receive praise.

*Do not give dogs
what is sacred;
do not throw
your pearls to pigs.
If you do,
they may trample
them under their feet,
and then turn and
tear you to pieces.*

JESUS OF NAZARETH

Matthew 7:6

The Ties That Bind and Gag*

On the other hand, giving to those we know, or those who "knew us when," can be among the most miserable serving experiences imaginable.

If you've tried giving to blood relatives and came away, well, bloody, know that you are not alone. In fact, you're in good company:

> Jesus left there and went to his hometown, accompanied by his disciples. When the Sabbath came, he began to teach in the synagogue, and many who heard him were amazed. "Where did this man get these things?" they asked. "What's this wisdom that has been given him, that he even does miracles! Isn't this the carpenter? Isn't this Mary's son and the brother of James, Joseph, Judas and Simon? Aren't his sisters here with us?" And they took offense at him.
>
> Jesus said to them, "Only in his hometown, among his relatives and in his own house is a prophet without honor."
>
> He could not do any miracles there, except lay his hands on a few sick people and heal them. (Mark 6:1–5)

If you feel like a prophet without honor (do your relatives only honor you when you show a profit?), be healed. Don't become a Becky.

What's a Becky? We thought you'd never ask.

---

*Chapter title appropriated from Erma Bombeck. Thank you, Mother Bombeck.

The little entourage
of friends and relatives
whom she
completely dominated
was fond of saying,
"Becky would give you
the shirt off her back."
And it was true.
The only trouble was
that she neglected
to take it off first,
and what you found
on your back
was not only
Becky's shirt
but Becky too.

MARGARET HALSEY

Don't Become a Becky

Herbert was
so benevolent,
so merciful a man that,
in his mistaken passion,
he would have held
an umbrella over a duck
in a shower of rain.

DOUGLAS JERROLD

Don't Become a Herbert, Either

*The bird thinks it is
an act of kindness
to give the fish
a lift in the air.*

RABIN-DRANATH TAGORE

Don't Be a Bird, Either

*When kindness
has left people,
even for a few moments,
we become
afraid of them
as if their reason
has left them.*

WILLA CATHER

Our Extended Family

Everything we've said about blood relatives is, of course, true for our extended family, as well. Our friends become our mothers-brothers-sisters-fathers-daughters-sons-cousins-aunts-uncles swinging from (and sometimes hanging on) our family tree.

No matter what we do, the most important thing to our family is that we *are*. The thought that we are there for others if needed can provide more comfort for them than our actual being there. The greatest gift we give our family, then, is simply *being*.

The most difficult gift to give our family? Giving *in*.

Which of you
if his son asks for bread,
will give him a stone?
Or if he asks for a fish,
will give him a snake?

JESUS OF NAZARETH

Matthew 7:9–10

*This is what
is hardest:
to close the open hand
because one loves.*

NIETZSCHE

*The first small sacrifice
of this sort
leads the way to others,
and a single hand's
turn given heartily
to the world's
great work helps one
amazingly with one's
own small tasks.*

LOUISA M. ALCOTT

Part Five

We Give to Good

*Service to a just cause
rewards the worker
with more real happiness
and satisfaction
than any other
venture of life.*

CARRIE CHAPMAN CATT

Give to Good? Good What?

Once again, what have you got? What good do you want to give to?

A good cause? Good government? Good works? Good organizations? Good earth? Good day?

We can, of course, give to all the goodness in life by sending light to it. When it comes to investing time, money, or energy, however, we must choose carefully.

You can give of yourself physically to *any* good you want, but you cannot give to *every* good you want.

As Jean Anouilh observed:

> One cannot weep for the entire world. It is beyond human strength. One must choose.

Choose.

Know that other givers are choosing other good to give to. Send them light. Send the light to the good you have not chosen. Then get busy.

Your chosen good awaits you.

*Charity begins
at home,
but should not
end there.*

THOMAS FULLER, M.D.

1732

*Live simply
that others may
simply live.*

ELIZABETH SEATON

Jesus sat down
opposite the place where
the offerings were put
and watched the crowd
putting their money
into the temple treasury.
Many rich people
threw in large amounts.
But a poor widow came
and put in two very small
copper coins [mites],
worth only a fraction of a penny.
Calling his disciples to him,
Jesus said,
"I tell you the truth,
this poor widow has put
more into the treasury
than all the others.
They all gave
out of their wealth;
but she, out of her poverty,
put in everything—
all she had to live on."

MARK 12:41–44

*Let your hand
feel for the afflictions
and distresses
of everyone,
and let your hand
give in proportion
to your purse;
remembering always
the estimation
of the widow's mite.*

GEORGE WASHINGTON

These are the times
that try men's souls.
The summer soldier
and the sunshine
patriot will,
in this crisis,
shrink from
the service
of their country;
but he that
stands it now,
deserves the love
and thanks of man
and woman.

THOMAS PAINE

*Philanthropy
is commendable,
but it must not cause
the philanthropist
to overlook the
circumstances
of economic injustice
which make
philanthropy necessary.*

DR. MARTIN LUTHER KING, JR.

The contents
of Sitting Bull's pockets
were often emptied
into the hands
of small,
ragged little boys,
nor could he understand
how so much wealth
should go brushing by,
unmindful of the poor.

ANNIE OAKLEY

*The white man
knows how
to make everything,
but he does not know
how to distribute it.*

SITTING BULL

Jean-Paul Sartre
(arriving in heaven):
It's not what I expected.

God: *What did you expect?*

Sartre: *Nothing.*

"SCTV"

Part Six

We Give to God

*Man discovers
his own wealth
when God comes
to ask gifts of him.*

RABIN-DRANATH TAGORE

Uh, God

When we talk of God; we skate on thin ice.

Allow us to quote from a great book—one we just happened to write ourselves: *LIFE 101*.

> We're going to take a clear, unequivocal and unambiguous position on God, religion, reincarnation, atheism, agnosticism and all that. Our clear, unambiguous and unequivocal position is this: We are clearly, unambiguously, and unequivocally *not* taking a position.

> We'd like to introduce a portion of life we call The Gap. The Gap is the area into which we put the many (often conflicting) beliefs people have about What's The Big Force Behind It All And How Does This Big Force Interact With Human Beings?

> The Gap can be any size, large or small. For some, it's a hairline crack; for others, it's vast enough to hold universes. We are not here to comment on the contents of anyone's Gap. The contents of your Gap are between you and whoever or whatever is in your Gap.

In calling an entire section of the book "We Give to God," we are not retreating from that, um, *diplomatic* policy. Please define God any way you choose, from Father God to Mother Nature to "the illimitable superior spirit who reveals himself in the slight details we are able to perceive with our frail and feeble mind" (Albert Einstein).

Whatever your view of God, giving to God—and to all that God has created—can be among the most satisfying forms of service.

All service ranks
the same with God.

ROBERT BROWNING

A Common Thread

In his book, *Oneness: Great Principles Shared by All Religions,* Jeffrey Moses points out that all religions have a common thread of giving, service, and charity:

CHRISTIANITY: It is more blessed to give than to receive.

TAOISM: Extend your help without seeking reward. Give to others and do not regret or begrudge your liberality. Those who are thus are good.

SIKHISM: In the minds of the generous contentment is produced.

ISLAM: The poor, the orphan, the captive— feed them for the love of God alone, desiring no reward, nor even thanks.

HINDUISM: Bounteous is he who gives to the beggar who comes to him in want of food and feeble.

JUDAISM: Blessed is he that considereth the poor: the Lord will deliver him in time of trouble.

BUDDHISM: The real treasure is that laid up by a man or woman through charity and piety, temperance and self control. The treasure thus hid is secure, and does not pass away.

Please enjoy the following common threads that weave the tapestry of our giving to God.*

*We don't for a *moment* think we can say it better than Jesus, Confucius, the Dalai Lama, Francis of Assisi, Benjamin Franklin, Fosdick, Homer, Paul, Mencken, Schweitzer, and, of course, Stradivarius.

*They serve God well,
who serve his
creatures.*

CAROLINE NORTON

*Every charitable act
is a stepping stone
towards heaven.*

HENRY WARD BEECHER

*A disciple
having asked for
a definition of charity,
the Master said:
Love One Another.*

CONFUCIUS

A new command
I give you:
Love one another.
As I have loved you,
so you must
love one another.
By this all men will know
that you are my disciples,
if you love one another.

JESUS OF NAZARETH

John 13:34–35

*We live very
close together.
So, our prime purpose
in this life is
to help others.
And if you can't
help them,
at least don't
hurt them.*

THE DALAI LAMA

*In the New Testament
it is taught that willing
and voluntary service
to others
is the highest duty and glory
in human life.
The men of talent
are constantly forced
to serve the rest.
They make the discoveries
and inventions,
order the battles,
write the books,
and produce the works of art.
The benefit and enjoyment
go to the whole.
There are those who joyfully
order their own lives
so that they may serve
the welfare of mankind.*

W. G. SUMNER

'Tis God gives skill,
But not without
men's hands:
He could not make
Antonio Stradivari's
violins
Without Antonio.

STRADIVARIUS

Lord, make me an
instrument of Your peace.
Where there is hatred
let me sow love;
where there is injury,
pardon;
where there is doubt,
faith;
where there is despair,
hope;
where there is darkness,
light;
and where there is sadness,
joy.

FRANCIS OF ASSISI

As you go,
preach this message:
"The kingdom of heaven
is near."
Heal the sick,
raise the dead,
cleanse those
who have leprosy,
drive out demons.
Freely you have
received,
freely give.

JESUS OF NAZARETH

Matthew 10:7–8

*Serving God is doing
good to man,
but praying is thought
an easier service
and therefore more
generally chosen.*

BENJAMIN FRANKLIN

Every good act is charity.
Your smiling in your brother's face,
is charity;
an exhortation of your fellowman
to virtuous deeds,
is equal to alms-giving;
your putting a wanderer
in the right road, is charity;
your assisting the blind, is charity;
your removing stones,
and thorns,
and other obstructions
from the road,
is charity;
your giving water to the thirsty,
is charity.
A man's true wealth hereafter,
is the good he does in this world
to his fellow-man.
When he dies,
people will say,
"What property has he
left behind him?"
But the angels will ask,
"What good deeds has he
sent before him?"

MOHAMMED

Be charitable
in your thoughts,
in your speech
and in your actions.
Be charitable
in your judgments,
in your attitudes
and in your prayers.
Think charitably
of your friends,
your neighbors,
your relatives and even
your enemies.
And if there be those whom
you can help in a material way,
do so in a quiet, friendly,
neighborly way,
as if it were the most
common and everyday
experience for you.
Tongues of men and angels,
gifts of prophecy
and all mysteries
and all knowledge
are as nothing
without charity.

CARDINAL HAYES

Spiritual energy
brings compassion
into the real world.
With compassion,
we see benevolently
our own human condition
and the condition
of our fellow beings.
We drop prejudice.
We withhold judgment.

CHRISTINA BALDWIN

Do not judge,
and you will not be judged.
Do not condemn,
and you will not
be condemned.
Forgive,
and you will be forgiven.
Give,
and it will be given to you.
For with the measure
you use,
it will be measured to you.

JESUS OF NAZARETH

Luke 6:37–38

Neither do people
light a lamp and put it
under a bowl.
Instead they put it
on its stand,
and it gives light to
everyone in the house.
In the same way,
let your light
shine before men,
that they may
see your good deeds
and praise
your Father in heaven.

JESUS OF NAZARETH

Matthew 5:15–16

If you love Jesus
work for justice.
Anybody can honk.

BUMPER STICKER

To give and not
to count the cost;
To fight and not
to heed the wounds;
To toil and not
to seek for rest;
To labour and not
ask for any reward
Save that of knowing
that we do Thy will.

IGNATIUS LOYOLA

1550

Make a joyful noise
unto the Lord,
all ye lands.
Serve the Lord
with gladness:
come before his presence
with singing.

PSALMS 100:1–2

*If anyone wants
to be first,
he must be
the very last,
and the servant of all.*

JESUS OF NAZARETH

Mark 9:35

One of the most amazing
things ever said
on this earth
is Jesus's statement:
"He that is greatest among
you shall be your servant."
Nobody has one chance
in a billion
of being thought really great
after a century has passed
except those who have been
the servants of all.
That strange realist
from Bethlehem knew that.

HARRY EMERSON FOSDICK

*For I was hungry and you
gave me something to eat,
I was thirsty and you
gave me something to drink,
I was a stranger and you
invited me in,
I needed clothes and you
clothed me,
I was sick and you
looked after me,
I was in prison and you
came to visit me.*

JESUS OF NAZARETH

Matthew 25:35–36

*By Jove the stranger
and the poor are sent,
And what to those
we give,
to Jove is lent.*

HOMER

Ninth Century B.C.

*God loveth
a cheerful giver.*

PAUL

2 Corinthians 9:7

*The Lord loveth
a cheerful giver.
He also accepteth
from a grouch.*

NOTICE IN A
CHURCH BULLETIN

*It is more
blessed to give
than to receive.*

JESUS OF NAZARETH

Acts 20:35

*'Tis always more blessed
to give than to receive;
for example,
wedding presents.*

H. L. MENCKEN

*There is no
higher religion
than human service.
To work for the
common good
is the greatest creed.*

ALBERT SCHWEITZER

Then choose
for yourselves this day
whom you will
serve. . . .
But as for me
and my household,
we will serve the Lord.

JOSHUA 24:15

Give a man a fish,
and you feed him
for a day.
Teach a man to fish,
and you feed him
for a lifetime.

CHINESE PROVERB

Part Seven

Tools for Givers

Do all the good you can,
By all the means you can,
In all the ways you can,
In all the places you can,
At all the times you can,
To all the people you can,
As long as ever you can.

JOHN WESLEY

Tools for Givers

Some of the techniques (tools) given in earlier books in THE LIFE 101 SERIES are particularly useful for givers. We present them again here in a slightly modified form with givers in mind.

Certainly don't limit yourself to these techniques: also use whatever methods you have found to work.

We discussed earlier the concept of sending the light for the highest good. This is a fundamental tool. Enclosed in this section are a few others.

If riches increase,
let thy mind hold pace
with them;
and think it not enough
to be liberal,
but munificent.

SIR THOMAS BROWNE

1690

Affirmations

Affirmation means to make firm, solid, more real. Thoughts—not very solid—when repeated over and over, become more and more firm. They become feelings, behaviors, experiences, and things. What we think about, we can become.

We affirm all the time. Sometimes we affirm negative things; sometimes we affirm positive things. In the words of Henry Ford, "If you think you can do a thing, or think you can't do a thing; you're right."

We, of course, are going to suggest that you consciously affirm the positive. Many of us already have the unconscious habit of affirming the negative. To change that, we quote Johnny Mercer, "You've got to accentuate the positive, eliminate the negative, latch on to the affirmative."

Affirmations usually begin with "I am . . ." "I am a happy, healthy, wealthy person." "I am joyful no matter what is happening around me." "I am loving and kind." If you're affirming for material things, it's a good idea to start even those with "I am . . ." "I am enjoying my new house." "I am creative and content in my new career." Affirmations are best expressed in the present. "I want a new car" affirms what? *Wanting* a new car. If what you want is *wanting* a new car, then that's a good affirmation. What you probably want, however, is the *car.* "I

*The greatest pleasure
I know
is to do a good action
by stealth,
and to have it
found out by accident.*

CHARLES LAMB

am safely and happily enjoying my beautiful new car." Affirm as though you already have what you want, even though you don't yet have it. (The operative word is "yet.")

No matter how "impossible" something may seem, put it into an affirmation form and give it a try. Say it, out loud, at least 100 times before you decide how "impossible" something might be. After 100 repetitions, you may find yourself quite comfortable with the idea.

You can write affirmations on paper and put them in places you will see them—on the bathroom mirror, refrigerator, next to your bed, on the car dashboard. You can also record them on endless-loop cassette tapes and play them in the background all day (and night) long.

A powerful technique is to say your affirmation while looking into your eyes in a mirror. All your limitations about the thing you're affirming are likely to surface, but persevere. Outlast the negative voices and doubting feelings. Plant the seed of your affirmation deep.

You can use affirmations written by other people, but remember that you are perfectly capable of creating your own. If you don't think so, start with the affirmation, "I am enjoying the success of the wonderful affirmations I create for myself." That should be the last affirmation anyone needs to write for you. (And you probably could have created a better one than *that.)*

*The measure of a man
is not the number
of his servants but in
the number of people
whom he serves.*

DR. PAUL D. MOODY

Affirmations work if you use them. The more you use them, the more they work. They can be used anywhere, anytime, while doing almost anything.

It's a good idea (a very good idea) to end all your affirmations with ". . . this or something better, for the highest good of all concerned."

The ". . . this or something better . . ." lets ten million come in when you merely asked for a million, and ". . . for the highest good of all concerned" assures that your affirmation is fulfilled in a way that's best for everyone.

Here are a few to get you started, but this is a very brief list. Learn to automatically turn all your wishes and wants into affirmations. Then start catching your negative thoughts, switching them around, and making affirmations out of them. By only slightly revising the negative chatter (changing "can't" to "can," "won't" to "will," "hate" to "love," etc.), you can turn all those formerly limiting voices into a staff of in-house affirmation writers.

> I am a joyful server.
>
> I am giving to love.
>
> I am happily sharing my abundance with others.
>
> Freely I am given to, and freely I give.
>
> I love to give; I give to love.
>
> I am so grateful to be of service.
>
> I am privileged to be of service.

His lord said unto him,
Well done, thou good
and faithful servant:
thou hast been faithful
over a few things,
I will make thee ruler
over many things:
enter thou into
the joy of thy lord.

JESUS OF NAZARETH

Matthew 25:21

Acceptance

Acceptance is such an important commodity, some have called it "the first law of personal growth." It could also be called "the first law of giving."

Acceptance is simply seeing something the way it is and saying, "That's the way it is."

Acceptance is not approval, consent, permission, authorization, sanction, concurrence, agreement, compliance, sympathy, endorsement, confirmation, support, ratification, assistance, advocating, backing, maintaining, authenticating, reinforcing, cultivating, encouraging, furthering, promoting, aiding, abetting, or even *liking* what is.

Acceptance is saying, "It is what it is, and what is is what is." Until we truly accept *everything*, we can never see clearly and seldom give appropriately. We will always be looking through the filters of musts, shoulds, ought-tos, have-tos, and prejudices.

When reality confronts our notion of what reality *should* be, reality always wins. (Drop something while believing gravity *shouldn't* make it fall. It falls anyway.) We don't like this (that is, we have trouble *accepting* this), so we either struggle with reality and become upset, or turn away from it and become unconscious. If you find yourself upset or unconscious—or alternating between the two—about something,

*I am not influenced
by the expectation
of promotion
or pecuniary reward.
I wish to be useful,
and every kind
of service necessary
for the public good,
becomes honorable
by being necessary.*

NATHAN HALE

you might ask yourself, "What am I not accepting about this?"

Acceptance is not a state of passivity or inaction. We are obviously not saying you can't change the world, right wrongs, or replace evil with good. Acceptance is the first step to successful service.

If you don't fully accept a situation precisely the way it is, you will have difficulty changing it. Moreover, if you don't fully accept the situation, you will never really know if the situation *should* be changed.

When you accept, you relax; you let go; you become patient. This is an enjoyable (and effective) place for either participation or departure. To stay and struggle (even for fun things: how many times have you tried *really hard* to have a good time?), or to run away in disgust and/or fear is not the most fulfilling way to live or give. It is, however, the inevitable result of non-acceptance.

Take a few moments and consider a situation you are not happy with—not your greatest burden in life, just a simple event about which you feel peeved. Now accept *everything* about the situation. Let it be the way it is. Because, after all, it *is* that way, is it not? Also, if you accept it, you will feel better about it.

After accepting it, and everything about it, you probably still won't *like* it, but you may stop hating and/or fearing it. At worst, you will hate it or fear it a little less.

*Blessed is he who
expects no gratitude,
for he shall not
be disappointed.*

W. C. BENNETT

That's the true value of acceptance: you feel better about life, and about yourself. Everything we've said about acceptance applies to things you have done (or failed to do) as well. In fact, everything we've said about acceptance applies *especially* to your judgments of you.

All the things you think you should have done that you didn't do, and all the things you did that you think you shouldn't have done, accept them. You did (or didn't) do them. That's reality. That's what happened. No changing the past. You can struggle with the past, or pretend it didn't happen, or you can accept it. We suggest the latter. A life of guilt, fear, and unconsciousness is, to say the least, not much fun. It also takes a lot of time and energy away from giving.

While you're at it, you might as well accept all your future transgressions against the shoulds, musts, and have-tos of this world. You will transgress. Not that we necessarily *endorse* transgression. We do, however, accept the fact that human beings *do* such things, and if you haven't yet accepted your humanity—with all the magnificence and folly inherent in that—now might be a good time to start.

Relax. Accept what's already taken place—whether done by you or something outside of you. Then look for the gift you are able to give and the best way of giving it. Acceptance lays the foundation for service.

There is a place
for everyone,
man and woman,
old and young,
hale and halt;
service in a thousand
forms is open.
There is no room
now for the dilettante,
the weakling,
for the shirker,
or the sluggard.
From the highest
to the humblest tasks,
all are of equal honor;
all have their part to play.

SIR WINSTON CHURCHILL

The Sanctuary

The imagination is a powerful tool. When used against us by creating unrealistic shoulds, musts, have-tos and other judgments, it can destroy our wealth utterly. When used for us, however, it can be one of the most vigorous creators of wealth—both inner and outer—in our lives.

The sanctuary is an inner structure that helps direct the imagination in wealthy ways. (If you have built a sanctuary while reading one of the other books in THE LIFE 101 SERIES, you can use this chapter to review, renew, and perhaps add to the sanctuary you already have.)

We call it a sanctuary. Some call it a workshop, or an inner classroom. You can call it whatever word gives you the sense of asylum, harbor, haven, oasis, shelter—a place you can go to learn your lessons in peace and harmony.

There are absolutely no limits to your sanctuary, although it's a good idea to put some limits on it. In this way, the sanctuary is a transitional point between the limitations of our physical existence and unlimitedness.

The sanctuary can be any size, shape, or dimension you choose—large and elaborate or small and cozy. It can be located anywhere—floating in space, on a mountain top, by an ocean, in a valley, anywhere. (You are welcome to combine all those, if you like.) The nice

*The noblest service comes
from nameless hands,
And the best servant
does his work unseen.*

OLIVER WENDELL HOLMES

thing about the sanctuary: you can change it or move it anytime—instantly.

The sanctuary can contain anything you choose. We'll suggest some things here, but consider this just the beginning of your shopping list. Before giving our design tips (you can consider us interior designers—with an emphasis on the word *interior),* we'll talk about ways in which you might want to build your sanctuary.

Some people will build theirs by simply reading the suggestions: as they read each, it's there. Others might read them over now for information, and then put on some soft music, close their eyes, and let the construction begin. Still others may want to make this an *active* process. With their eyes closed (and being careful not to bump into too much furniture), they might physically move as each area of the sanctuary is built and used. All—or any combination—of these are, of course, fine.

While reading through our suggestions, you will probably get ideas for additions or alterations. By all means make notes of these, or simply incorporate them as you go. Have we gotten across the idea that this is *your* sanctuary? Okay, let's go.

Entryway. This is a door or some device that responds only to you and lets only you enter. (We'll suggest a way to bring others into your sanctuary in a moment.)

Light. Each time you enter your sanctuary, a pure, white light cascades over you, sur-

Rather than love,
than money,
than fame,
give me truth.

THOREAU

rounding, filling, protecting, blessing, and healing you—for your highest good, and the highest good of all concerned.

Main Room. Like the living room of a house or the lobby of a hotel, this is the central area. From here, there are many directions to go and many things to explore.

People Mover. This is a device to move people in and out of your sanctuary. No one ever enters without your express permission and invitation. You can use an elevator, conveyor belt, *Star Trek* beam-me-up device, or anything else that moves people. Let there be a white light at the entry of the mover as well, so that as people enter and leave your sanctuary, they are automatically surrounded, filled, protected, and healed by that white light, and only that which is for their highest good and the highest good of all concerned is taking place.

Information Retrieval System. This is a method of getting any kind of information—providing, of course, it's for your highest good (and the highest good of all concerned) that you have it. The information retrieval system can be a computer screen, a staff of librarians, a telephone, or any other device from which you feel comfortable asking questions and getting answers.

Video Screen. This is a video (or movie, if you like) screen in which you can view various parts of your life— past, present, or future. The screen has a white light around it. When you

This is the true joy in life,
the being used for a purpose
recognized by yourself
as a mighty one;
the being thoroughly
worn out
before you are thrown
on the scrap heap;
the being a force of nature
instead of a feverish
selfish little clod
of ailments and grievances
complaining that the world
will not devote itself
to making you happy.

GEORGE BERNARD SHAW

see images you don't like or don't want to encourage, the light is off. When the screen displays images you want to affirm, the light glows. (Those who are old enough to remember Sylvania's Halo of Light television know just what we mean.)

Ability Suits. This is a closet of costumes that, when worn, give you the instant ability to do anything you want to do—great actor, successful writer, perfect lover, eager learner, Master of your Universe; any and all are available to you. When you're done with an ability suit, just throw it on the floor in front of the closet—ability suits have the ability to hang themselves up.

Ability Suit Practice Area. This is a place you can try new skills—or improve upon old ones—while wearing your ability suits. Leave lots of room, because there's an ability suit for flying and another for space travel. In your sanctuary, not even the sky's a limit.

Health Center. Here the healing arts of all the ages—past, present, future; traditional and alternative—are gathered in one place. All are devoted to your greater health. The health center is staffed with the most competent health practitioners visualization can buy. Who is the most healing being you can imagine? That's who runs your center.

Service Center. Here is a place where you can gather together other givers and swap sto-

And I will ask
the Father,
and he will give you
another Counselor
to be with you
forever—
the Spirit of truth.
The world
cannot accept him,
because it neither
sees him nor knows him.
But you know him,
for he lives with you
and will be in you.

JESUS OF NAZARETH

John 14:16–17

ries, exchange encouragement, and give and receive love.

Playroom. Here, all the toys you ever wanted—as a child or as an adult—are gathered. There's lots of room—and time—to play with each. As with ability suits, you never have to worry about "putting your toys away." They put themselves away.

Sacred Room. This is a special sanctuary within your sanctuary. You can go there for meditation, contemplation, or special inner work.

Master Teacher. This is your ideal teacher, the being with whom you are the perfect student. The Master Teacher (or MT for short) knows everything about you (has always been with you, in fact). The MT also knows all you need to learn, the perfect timing for your learning it, and the ideal way of teaching it to you.

You don't *create* a Master Teacher—that's already been done. You *discover* your Master Teacher. To meet your Master Teacher, simply walk over to your people mover, ask for your Master Teacher to come forth, and from the pure, white light of your people mover comes your Master Teacher.

(We'll leave you two alone for a while. More uses for the sanctuary later. See you both in the next chapter!)

If you have much
give of your wealth,
if you have little
give of your heart.

ARAB PROVERB

Using Your Sanctuary for Giving and Serving

Once built in your imagination, the sanctuary is accessible and available as any other memory or inner creation. Accessing your sanctuary doesn't even require closing your eyes, although for extended work in the sanctuary many people prefer it.

What follow are just a few suggestions on how to use various aspects of your sanctuary for greater giving and service. Obviously, this is just a beginning. Use your creativity. Follow your heart. Ask your Master Teacher. The uses of your sanctuary for giving and service are almost limitless.

People Mover. You can use this device to invite people you'd like to give to into your sanctuary. Just as no one is allowed in your sanctuary without your express permission and invitation, so too will no one come into your sanctuary without his or her permission. If you want to work with someone, invite them in, and if they don't show up—let it go. Move on to someone or something else. For whatever reason, that person has made the choice not to come into your sanctuary. Honor his or her choice. Later, you might ask again. If a person won't come in, say, three times in a row, you may want to discuss it with your Master Teacher. Perhaps the person is not ready to receive; perhaps you're not the one destined to

Love sought is good,
but giv'n unsought
is better.

SHAKESPEARE

give at this time. Most people do come in (the vast majority do: being invited into a sanctuary is a great blessing). When you're working with people in your sanctuary, it's important to give to them *for their highest good and the highest good of all concerned.* Don't impose what *you* think would be best for them. You can certainly *suggest* certain activities, and if they accept, fine. You can also give them a tour of your sanctuary and see what appeals to them. Trust the inner knowing of the people you serve. The sanctuary is a very effective place for giving to people who are difficult to be with in person (the "representative" they send to the sanctuary is usually the "kinder, gentler" version of themselves).

Information Retrieval System. A great place to gather information useful in your service and giving.

Video Screen. As the white light around the video screen glows, see yourself joyfully giving and successfully serving.

Ability Suits and Ability Suit Practice Area. One of your ability suits has a giant G on it—the ability suit of Super Giver. (If you also have an ability suit with a giant S on it—for Super Server, don't let the Superman people see you flying around in it—they are *so* touchy about their trademark.) In the ability suit practice area, Super Giver suit in place, you can practice giving of all types and kinds. You can also use any of the other ability suits (balance, patience, compassion, energy) to help you in

*Charity is twice
blessed—
it blesses the one
who gives
and the one
who receives.*

your giving. More than one ability suit at a time is fine. You can also put on ability suits before entering real-life situations (it only takes a second) where any of these abilities may be required.

Health Center. Use the health center not only to keep yourself healthy, but also invite other people you would like to serve into your health center for healing.

Playroom. This is a great place to awaken the child within yourself, and to give to the child within all those you give to.

Sacred Room. Perhaps the people you give to would like to do some meditation, contemplation, or other spiritual work. The sacred room is an ideal place for that. You can be with them, or they may prefer some time alone.

Service Center. Here is a place to "hang out" with all your fellow great givers, past and present, known and unknown, famous and infamous.

Master Teacher. The Master Teacher is one of the most practical and valuable tools for any giver. The Master Teacher is an absolute expert on giving. Ask your Master Teacher the best way to handle challenging situations of service. Introduce your Master Teacher to people you are working with (within your sanctuary—there's no point turning your life into a giver's version of *Harvey*). While serving in "real life," listen for the voice of your Master Teacher. That voice is a direct connection to some of your greatest powers of giving.

*By compassion
we make others'
misery our own,
and so,
by relieving them,
we relieve ourselves
also.*

SIR THOMAS BROWNE

1642

For Giving

Forgiving means "for giving"—*for*, in favor of; *giving,* to give. When you forgive another, to whom do you give? The other? Sometimes. Yourself? Always. To forgive another is being *in favor of giving* to yourself and to others.

In addition, most of us judge ourselves more harshly and more often than we judge others. It's important to forgive ourselves for all the things we hold against ourselves.

There is a third thing to forgive: the fact that we ever judged in the first place. When we judge, we leave our happiness behind—sometimes *way* behind. We know this, and we judge ourselves for having judged in the first place.

The layers of forgiveness, then, are two: first, the person we judged (ourselves or another); and, second, ourselves for having judged in the first place.

The technique? Simple. So simple, that some people doubt its effectiveness and don't try it. We urge you to try it.

Say to yourself, "I forgive _____ [name of the person, place, or thing you judged, including yourself] for _____ [the "transgression"]. I forgive myself for judging _____ [same person, place, or thing, including yourself] for _____ [what you judged]."

Da da da (that is)
Be subdued,
Give,
Be merciful.

BRIHADARANYAKA UPANISHAD

800–500 B.C.

♥ ♥ ♥

That's it. Simple, but amazingly effective. You can say it out loud, or say it to yourself. But, please, do say it.

If you have a lot to forgive one person for, you might want to invite that person into your sanctuary and forgive the person there. (Ask your Master Teacher to come along, if you choose.)

That's all there is to forgiveness. Simple but powerful. How powerful? Give it five minutes. See what happens.

*Not he who
has much is rich,
but he who
gives much.*

ERICH FROMM

For Getting

After you've forgiven the transgression and the judgment, there's only one thing to do: forget them. Whatever "protection" you think you may gain from remembering all your past grievances is far less important than the balm of forgetting.

What's the value in forgetting? It's all in the word: for getting—to be in favor of getting, of receiving.

If you have a clenched fist, it is difficult to receive. If you let go and open the fist, you have a hand. Then it's easy to receive. And to give.

We sometimes think that shaking a fist (threateningly, with all the remembered transgressions) is the way to get something. A shaking fist tends to beget a shaking (or swinging) fist.

To receive, for give. To get, for get. To give, for give and for get.

The space in your consciousness (mind, body, emotions) that's remembering a grievance is locked into remembering hurt, pain, anger, betrayal, and disappointment. Who on earth wants to remember *that?* Let it go. For give it away. Then *for get* something new and better (light-er) in its place. Then you have something more valuable inside you from which to give.

Heal the memories. Forgive the past. Then forget it. Let it go. It is not worth remember-

*Charity sees the need,
not the cause.*

GERMAN PROVERB

ing. None of it's worth remembering. What's worth *experiencing* and *giving* is the joy of this moment. Sound good?

To get it, for get.

For get to give.

*It's so much easier
to do good
than to be good.*

B. C. FORBES

Commitments

As a giver, you will be called upon to commit your time, money, service, and support. To the degree that it's possible, keep those agreements. This makes you a better giver and makes those you give to more willing to receive.

You will also find that some of the people you make agreements with will not keep them. If you want to be a happy giver, forgive it, forget it, and move on with your giving.

When we make a commitment, we "give our word." Giving something as valuable and as powerful as our word should not be taken lightly. When we don't fulfill our word, a part of us begins to mistrust ourselves. Over time, the effects of broken commitments build up. One begins to have a serious case of self-doubt and discomfort.

This self-doubt feeds the unworthiness, causing tiredness, confusion, lack of clarity, and a general sense of "I can't do it."

Parallel to this disintegration in our relationship with ourselves is the deterioration of our relationships with others. If you make a series of commitments and don't keep them, people—at best—don't trust you. At worst, it's a great deal of *Sturm und Drang*—hurt feelings, anger, betrayal, abandonment, etc.

Keeping this in mind, it's easy to see that if you've been, shall we say, *freewheeling* in your

That sir which serves
and seeks for gain,
And follows
but for form,
Will pack
when it begins to rain,
And leave thee
in the storm.

SHAKESPEARE

commitments—either with yourself or with others—you have plowed, irrigated, and well fertilized the soil in which negative thinking thrives.

To reverse this—and prevent future fertilization—we have a few suggestions:

1. Don't make commitments you're not sure you can keep. If you're not sure, say you're not sure. If a definite maybe is not good enough, it's better to tell the other person no.

2. Only make commitments that are important to you. If a commitment is important enough, you'll keep it. If it's not important enough, don't make it.

3. Learn to say no. Don't make commitments that are important to someone else but not important to you just because you're afraid of "hurting their feelings." In doing this, you will either (A) break the commitment later, causing more hurt feelings, or (B) keep the agreement, hurting your own feelings. It's better to say "No, thank you" up front.

4. Communicate. As soon as you know you're not going to be able to keep a commitment, let the other person know. Even if you *think* you won't be able to keep it, let the other person know. And don't just say, "Sorry, can't make it." Renegotiate. Changing a commitment is asking for a favor. Do it nicely.

5. Write down your commitments with others. Keep a calendar and note your appointments. This (A) helps you remember them and (B) avoids scheduling conflicts.

The last temptation
is the greatest treason:
To do the right deed
for the wrong reason.

T. S. ELIOT

6. Write down commitments with yourself. Write this on the first page of your calendar: "All commitments with myself will be put in writing. Everything else is just a good idea." This keeps you from thinking the "good idea" to go jogging tomorrow at 6 a.m. is actually a commitment. If it is a commitment, write "Jogging, 6 a.m." in your calendar. And do it.

7. Declare everything finished. If you have a half-dozen half-read books lying around open, gathering dust, declare your reading of them finished. Put book marks in them and put them away. Tell yourself, "I'm done with this for now." You can always go back and pick them up again, but for now, release yourself from any implied commitment you have with yourself and have not finished. The same works with commitments with others. When you know you're not going to be taking part in something people expect you to be taking part in, let them know that, until further notice, you won't be there. It's amazing how much energy declaring things finished can free up within you.

8. Forgive yourself. Forgive yourself for any broken agreements in the past. Forgive yourself for judging yourself for having broken those agreements. While you're at it, forgive yourself for breaking any agreements you may make in the future.

It may help you keep your agreements—and not make agreements you don't plan to keep—if you understand the four primary reasons people break agreements:

*Do not ask me
to be kind;
just ask me
to act as though
I were.*

JULES RENARD

1. *Approval.* We say we'll do something we really don't want to do because we're afraid someone might disapprove of us—then we don't have time to keep all the conflicting agreements. In addition, we lose our own self-approval in the process.

2. *Comfort.* It's more comfortable not to keep the commitment. This is actually a false sense of comfort. If, for example, you want to lose weight and it *seems* more comfortable to go off your diet and eat some cake, the resulting post-cake discomfort is likely to be greater than the discomfort caused by not eating the cake in the first place.

3. *Rebellion.* Breaking agreements for rebels is a knee-jerk reaction to feeling hemmed in, limited, or tied down in any way. Rebels especially feel rebellion toward (A) authority figures and (B) ultimatums. Unfortunately, rebelling against the "doctor's orders" (an authority figure issuing ultimatums!) can be fatal.

4. *Unconsciousness.* Unconsciousness is a very important reason that people break agreements. There are other important things to say about this, but we forgot them. Maybe we'll remember later. Uh, yeah.

Keeping agreements (and not making agreements you don't plan to keep) is a good way to learn about your need for other people's approval and how to replace it with self-approval, how to expand your "comfort zone" so you'll have more freedom, and how to move from

*Charity begins
at home,
and generally dies
from lack
of outdoor exercise.*

automatic, unthinking rebellion into conscious, voluntary cooperation. And how to stay awake, too!

The second part of our little "secret of happiness" is simple—whenever anyone breaks an agreement with you, let it go. In your mind, let the other person out of the agreement at once. Imagine that the person called with the best reason and apology in the world.

Let it go.

Expecting human beings to keep their agreements is (A) not realistic and (B) an invitation to irritation.

When someone—especially someone important to you—breaks an agreement it may bring back earlier images and feelings of being let down, betrayed, and abandoned. Use the opportunity to heal these memories from the past, not to add further injury to yourself in the present. That's good giving.

Then Peter said,
"Silver or gold
I do not have,
but what I have
I give you."

ACTS 3:6

Behold,
I do not
give lectures or
a little charity,
When I give
I give myself.

WALT WHITMAN

Sometimes
I sits and thinks
and sometimes
I just sits.

Meditate, Contemplate, or Just Sits

As we give, it's important to remember our center, our being, the source of all our service. There are many techniques for doing this— meditation, contemplation, or you can always "just sits."

Whenever you meditate, contemplate, pray, do spiritual exercises, or "just sits," it's good to ask the white light to surround, fill, and protect you, knowing only that which is for your highest good and the highest good of all concerned will take place during your meditation.

Before starting, prepare your physical environment. Arrange not to be disturbed. Unplug the phone. Put a note on the door. Wear ear plugs if noises might distract you. (We like the soft foam-rubber kind sold under such trade names as E.A.R., HUSHER, and DECIDAMP.) Take care of your bodily needs. Have some water nearby if you get thirsty, and maybe some tissues, too.

Contemplation is thinking *about* something, often something of an uplifting nature. You could contemplate any of the hundreds of quotes or ideas in this book. Often, when we hear a new and potentially useful idea, we say, "I'll have to think about that." Contemplation is a good time to "think about that," to consider

*[The sun] gives light
as soon as he rises.*

BENJAMIN FRANKLIN

the truth of it, to imagine the changes and improvements it might make in your life.

Or, you could contemplate a nonverbal object, such as a flower, or a concept, such as God. The idea of contemplation is to set aside a certain amount of quiet time to think about just *that,* whatever you decide "that" will be.

Meditation. There are so many techniques of meditation, taught by so many organizations, that it's hard to define the word properly. We'll give a capsule summary of some techniques from John-Roger's book, *Inner Worlds of Meditation.* (For more complete descriptions, you can get the book for $7 postpaid, from Mandeville Press, Box 3935, Los Angeles, CA 90051.)

You might want to try various meditations to see what they're like. With meditation, please keep in mind that *you'll never know until* you do it. We may somehow like to think we know what the effects of a given meditation will be just by reading the description, and that, in fact, is exactly what happens. We think we know; we don't *really* know. We suggest you try it, gain the experience, and decide from that more stable base of knowledge what is best for you at this time. And please remember to "call in the light" before beginning. We suggest you do not do these meditations while driving a car, operating dangerous machinery, or where you need to be alert.

*If we do not
lay out ourselves
in the service of mankind
whom should we serve?*

ABIGAIL ADAMS

Breathing Meditation. Sit comfortably, close your eyes, and simply be aware of your breath. Follow it in and out. Don't "try" to breathe; don't consciously alter your rhythm of breathing; just follow the breath as it naturally flows in and out. If you get lost in thoughts, return to your breath. This can be a very refreshing meditation—twenty minutes can feel like a night's sleep. It's also especially effective when you're feeling emotionally upset.

Tones. Some people like to add a word or sound to help the mind focus as the breath goes in and out. Some people use *one* or *God* or AUM (OHM) or *love*. These—or any others— are fine. As you breathe in, say to yourself, mentally, "love." As you breathe out, "love." A few other tones you might want to try:

- **HU.** HU is an ancient sound for the higher power. One of the first names humans ever gave to a supreme being was HU. Some good words begin with HU: *humor, human, hub* (the center), *hug, huge, hue, humus* ("The Good Earth"), *humble,* and, of course, *hula.* HU is pronounced "Hugh." You can say it silently as you breathe in, and again as you breathe out. Or, you can pronounce the letter H on the inhale and the letter U on the exhale. You might also try saying HU out loud as you exhale, but don't do it out loud more than fifteen times in one sitting; the energies it produces can be powerful.

You give but little
when you give
of your possessions.
It is when you give
of yourself
that you truly give.

KAHLIL GIBRAN

- **ANI-HU.** This tone brings with it compassion, empathy, and unity. You can chant it silently (ANI on the inhale, HU on the exhale) or out loud (ANI-HU on the exhale). It makes a lovely group chant and tends to harmonize the group—in more ways than one.

- **HOO.** This can be used like the HU. Some people prefer it. It's one syllable, pronounced like the word *who*.

- **RA.** RA is a tone for bringing great amounts of physical energy into the body. You can do it standing or sitting. Standing tends to bring in more energy. Take a deep breath and, as you exhale, chant, out loud, "ERRRRRRRRAAAAAAAAA" until your air runs out. Take another deep breath and repeat it; then again. After three RAs, breathe normally for a few seconds. Then do another set of three, pause, then another set of three. We suggest you don't do more than three sets of three at any one time.

- **SO-HAWNG.** The SO-HAWNG meditation is a good one to use when your mind wants to do one thing and your emotions another. SO-HAWNG tends to unify the two, getting them on the same track. This tone is done silently. You breathe in on SO and out on HAWNG. Try it with your eyes closed for about five minutes and see how you feel. You may feel ready

*Who serves
a good lord
lives always in luxury.*

POEM OF THE CID

Twelfth Century

to accomplish some task you've been putting off for a long time.

- **THO.** THO is a tone of healing. The correct pronunciation of it is important. Take a deep breath, and as you breathe out say, "THooooo." The TH is accented; it's a sharp, percussive sound (and it may tickle your upper lip). It's followed by "ooooooo" as an extended version of the word *oh*. To do the THO meditation, sit comfortably, close your eyes, inhale and exhale twice, take a third deep breath, and on the third exhale, say, "THooooo." Repeat three times this series of three breaths with THO aloud on the third breath. That's enough. It's powerful. Feel the healing energies move through your body. You can also chant THO inwardly as a formal meditation or any time during the day, even while doing something else. (But, again, as with all meditations, not while driving a car or operating potentially dangerous equipment.)

Flame Meditation. This uses the power of fire to dissolve negativity. Put a candle on a table and sit so you can look directly into the flame, not down on it. Allow your energy to flow *up* and *out* into the candle. You may feel negativity or have negative thoughts. Don't pay any attention to their content; just release them into the flame. If you feel your energy dropping back down inside of you as though

A man makes no noise
over a good deed,
but passes on
to another as a vine
to bear grapes
again in season.

MARCUS AURELIUS

Second Century

you were going into a trance, blow out the candle and stop the meditation. The idea is to keep the energy flowing up and out and into the flame. Do it for no more than five minutes to start. See how you feel for a day or so afterward. You may have more vivid dreams. If you feel fine otherwise, you might try it for longer periods. Twenty minutes a day would be a lot.

Water Meditation. Take some water in a clear glass, hold it between your hands (without your hands touching each other), and simply look down into the glass. Observe whatever you observe. You may see colors. You may see energy emanating from your hands. You may just see yourself holding a glass of water. Observe the water for five minutes, gradually working up to fifteen. Drink the water at the end of the meditation. Your energies have made it a "tonic," giving you whatever you may need at that time. As an experiment, you can take two glasses, each half-filled with tap water. Set one aside, and do the water meditation with the other. Then taste each. Don't be surprised if the one you "charged" tastes different.

E. The E sound is chanted out loud after meditation to "ground" you and bring your focus back to the physical. It's a steady "Eeeeeeeeeeee" as though you were pronouncing the letter E. It begins at the lower register of your voice, travels to the upper range, then back down again in one breath. You begin as a bass, go through tenor, alto, onto soprano, and back to bass again. As you do this, imagine that the sound is in your feet when

No person
was ever honored
for what he received.
Honor has been
the reward
for what he gave.

CALVIN COOLIDGE

you're in the lower register, gradually going higher in your body as your voice goes higher, finally reaching the top of your head at the highest note of the eeee, and then back down your body as the voice lowers. If you try it, you'll see that it's far easier to do than it is to explain. Do two or three E sounds after each meditation session.

♥ ♥ ♥

These tones and meditations have worked for many people. We don't ask you to *believe* they work. We simply ask you, if you like, to try them and see what happens. If they do work, you don't need belief; you have knowledge. Your results will dictate whether you'll use them often, sometimes, seldom, or never.

Some may work better for you than others; that's only natural. Use the ones that work best for you now and, every so often, return to the others to see if they will offer more.

Some people think meditation takes time *away* from physical accomplishments such as giving and service. Taken to extremes, of course, that's true. Most people, however, find that meditation *creates* more time than it *takes*.

Meditation is for rest, healing, balance and information. All these are helpful in the attainment of a goal, or the giving of a gift. Here's an additional technique you might want to add to

When we grow old,
there can only be
one regret—
not to have given
enough of ourselves.

ELEONORA DUSE

your meditation. It's designed to make both the meditation and the time outside of meditation more effective.

One of the primary complaints people have about meditating is, "My thoughts won't leave me alone." Perhaps the mind is trying to communicate something valuable. If the thought is something to do, write it down (or record it on a tape recorder). Then return to the meditation. This allows the mind to move onto something else—such as meditation, for example.

As the "to do" list fills, the mind empties. If the thought, "Call the homeless shelter," reappears, you need only tell the mind, "It's on the list. You can let that one go." And it will. (It is important, however, to *do* the things on the list—or at least to consider them from a non-meditative state. If you don't, the mind will not pay any more attention to your writing it down than you do, and will continue to bring it up, over and over.)

When finished meditating, not only will you have had a better meditation, you will also have a "to do" list that is very useful. One insight gleaned during meditation might save *hours,* perhaps *days* of unnecessary work. That's what we mean when we say—from a purely practical point of view—meditation can make more time than it takes.

No one would remember
the Good Samaritan
if he only had
good intentions.
He had money as well.

MARGARET THATCHER

Seeding and Tithing

Seeding and tithing are two important aspects of giving. One is saying "please"; the other is saying "thank you."

Seeding and tithing are acknowledging the *source* of our good, our abundance. The source can be represented by whatever we choose—whichever organization or person represents the highest good we know. The acknowledgement is in the form of *money*.

Money. Yes, money. Giving away *money* shows we *really mean it*. Just *whom* does it show we really mean it? Why, *ourselves,* of course. And it shows the comfort zone, too. There's little the comfort zone has a tighter hold on than the purse strings. If you can give away *money*—in set amounts and at regular intervals—your mastery of the comfort zone is well under way, and your giving moves into high gear.

Seeding is giving money away *before* you achieve something. As its name implies, it is *planting a seed*. What would it be worth to you—in terms of hard cash—to have your service in a specific area be successful? Seed from one to ten percent of that amount. How do you seed? Send a check to the organization or person that represents—in your estimation—the highest power for good, and let it go.

Don't tell *anyone* that you have seeded for something until *after* you have achieved it.

*Many people give
a tenth to the Lord—
a tenth of what
they ought to give.*

Tithing is giving away ten percent of your material increase. If you make $1,000, give $100 of it away. If someone gives you something worth $1,000, give $100 (in cash or valuable asset) away.

Why? By tithing, you make a statement of abundance to yourself. You are saying, "Thank you. I have more than I need." To consistently give away ten percent of your increase indicates—through action—that you are a conscientious user of energy. Those who waste energy, it seems, are given less and less. Those who make good use of it are given more and more. Tithing demonstrates you are a good manager of resources.

Seeding and tithing in set amounts on a regular basis keeps your abundance flowing. From that abundance and that overflow, you can give even more than the amount you seed and tithe. In order to give, however, you must have a flow of abundance, and we have found this flow of abundance is best obtained by seeding and tithing.

Where you give your money is not important. If you have no spiritual or religious affiliation (the traditional depository of seeding and tithing), you can give to your favorite charity or social cause. Just so it represents to you the *highest* and *best* work being done on the planet, any organization—or person—is fine.

♥ ♥ ♥

Woe to you, teachers
of the law and Pharisees,
you hypocrites!
You give a tenth
of your spices—
mint, dill and cummin.
But you have neglected
the more important matters
of the law—
justice, mercy
and faithfulness.
You should have practiced
the latter,
without neglecting
the former.

JESUS OF NAZARETH
Matthew 23:23

One more thought: if you give begrudgingly, it will be given unto you begrudgingly. If you give joyfully, it will be given unto you joyfully.

Don't wait to give, however, until you can do it joyfully. It's a mechanical process. Being given to begrudgingly is better than not having either happen at all.

*A lot of people
are willing to give God
the credit,
but not too many
are willing to give him
the cash.**

*We don't know where this one came from, but our bets are on "Laugh-In."

Giving away a fortune is taking Christianity too far.

CHARLOTTE BINGHAM

*Prayer carries us
half way to God,
fasting brings us
to the door of His palace,
and alms-giving
procures us admission.*

THE KORAN

Sacrifice

You would be far happier if you gave up certain things. This may not be easy for you. We nonetheless suggest you give them up—go cold turkey—starting right now, this minute, before you turn the page.

Give is an up word. *Up* is an up word. Put them together, and people get awfully down. "I'm not going to give up *anything*. And *sacrifice*. That's even *worse* than giving up. Sacrifice means giving up something *really* good."

The things we think you'd be better off sacrificing are things such as greed, lust, hurt, judgments, demands, spoiledness, envy, jealousy, vindictiveness.

Did you think we were going to ask you to give up good stuff? Most people think that sacrifice means giving up only the good stuff. Not so. The negative stuff, the cold stuff, the hard stuff—you can sacrifice those, too.

And you can give them up. Surrender them to the higher part of yourself. Surround them with light. Let them go.

You don't need them anymore.

Giving these things up will give immeasurable gifts to you and all those you come into contact with.

*In about
the same degree
as you are helpful,
you will be happy.*

KARL REILAND

Part Eight

We Give to Love

There are those
who give with joy,
and that joy is their reward.
And there are those
who give with pain,
and that pain
is their baptism.
And there are those
who give and know not
pain in giving,
nor do they seek joy,
nor give with mindfulness
of virtue;
They give as in yonder valley
the myrtle breathes
its fragrance into space.
Through the hands
of such as these God speaks,
and from behind their eyes
He smiles upon the earth.

KHALIL GIBRAN

We Give to . . .

At first, we give to receive.

Later, we give because giving feels good.

Eventually, we give because, well, that's just what we do.

At that time, the giver and the gift become one.

♥ ♥ ♥

And now, we turn the remainder of our book over to the thoughts of giving hearts and loving minds—from Jefferson to Jesus, from Nietzsche to Bob Hope—who tell us of the gift of giving to love.

Getters generally don't
get happiness;
givers get it.
You simply give to others
a bit of yourself—
a thoughtful act,
a helpful idea,
a word of appreciation,
a lift over a rough spot,
a sense of understanding,
a timely suggestion.
You take something
out of your mind,
garnished in kindness
out of your heart,
and put it
into the other fellow's
mind and heart.

CHARLES H. BURR

*There never was
a person who did
anything worth doing
who did not receive
more than he gave.*

HENRY WARD BEECHER

The luxury
of doing good
surpasses every other
personal enjoyment.

JOHN GAY

1685–1732

*Every human mind
feels pleasure in
doing good to another.*

THOMAS JEFFERSON

As the purse is emptied,
the heart is filled.

VICTOR HUGO

*The quality of mercy
is not strained,
It droppeth as the
gentle rain from heaven
Upon the place beneath:
it is twice blessed;
It blesseth
him that gives and
him that takes.*

SHAKESPEARE

Peace I leave with you;
my peace
I give you.
I do not give to you
as the world gives.
Do not let your hearts
be troubled and
do not be afraid.

JESUS OF NAZARETH

John 14:27

If you haven't got any charity in your heart, you have the worst kind of heart trouble.

BOB HOPE

*He who cannot
give anything away
cannot feel anything
either.*

NIETZSCHE

Give all to love;
Obey thy heart.

EMERSON

*Kindness
is never wasted.
If it has no effect
on the recipient,
at least it benefits
the bestower.*

*Kindness can become
its own motive.
We are made kind
by being kind.*

ERIC HOFFER

*Service is nothing but
love in work clothes.*

A cheerful giver
does not count the cost
of what he gives.
His heart is set
on pleasing and cheering
him to whom
the gift is given.

JULIAN OF NORWICH

Revelations of Divine Love

1373

The greatest reward
for serving others is
the satisfaction found
in your own heart.

The roots of happiness
grow deepest
in the soil
of service.

One glorious chain
of love.

SAMSON R. HIRSCH

Don't give till it hurts—
give till it feels good.

*Charity is
that which opens
in each heart
a little Heaven.*

MATTHEW PRIOR

*Kindness is the insignia
of a loving heart.*

Life is made up,
not of great sacrifices
or duties,
but of little things,
in which smiles
and kindness,
and small obligations
given habitually,
are what preserve
the heart and
secure comfort.

WILLIAM DAVY

A man's true wealth
is the good he does
in this world.

Don't expect
to enjoy life
if you keep your
milk of human kindness
all bottled up.

*The fragrance always
remains in the hand
that gives the rose.*

HEDA BEJAR

Let us open up
our natures,
throw wide the doors
of our hearts and
let in the sunshine
of good will
and kindness.

O. S. MARDEN

*The natural dignity
of our work,
its unembarrassed
kindness,
its insight into life,
its hold on science—
for these privileges,
and for all that they
bring with them,
up and up,
high over the top
of the tree,
the very heavens open,
preaching thankfulness.*

STEPHEN PAGET

*See first that
you yourself
deserve to be a giver,
and an
instrument of giving.
For in truth it is life
that gives unto life—
while you,
who deem yourself
a giver,
are but a witness.*

KHALIL GIBRAN

I no longer
call you servants,
because a servant
does not know
his master's business.
Instead,
I have called you friends,
for everything
that I learned
from my Father
I have made
known to you.

JESUS OF NAZARETH

John 15:15

For Further Study:
Organizations Founded by
John-Roger

This is Peter, stepping out of my co-author character, to tell you about some of the organizations founded by John-Roger.

J-R must like founding organizations. I certainly *hope* he likes founding organizations—he's founded enough of them. It's probably more accurate to say that organizations formed *around* John-Roger; he stands still for a while and teaches, and the people listening to him form organizations by which these teachings can be shared with others.

The organizations range from the secular to the spiritual—that is, some are of The Gap, and some are not. I'll list them in approximate order of Gap-ness—starting with the purely secular.

Now that you've had a taste of J-R's teachings (through this book), you might want to explore some more. (In this book we have barely scratched the surface—he's been at it nonstop for the past thirty years.)

The Heartfelt Foundation is dedicated to service. They do various community projects, large and small, all over the world. If you'd like to take part—or organize a service project in your community—give them a call. The Heartfelt Foundation also presents Service Trainings; workshops in which people learn to be of greater service to themselves, their families, their communities, the world, and humanity at large. For further information, please write the Heartfelt Foundation. 2101 Wilshire Blvd., Santa Monica, CA 90403; 310-828-0535.

Institute for Individual and World Peace. Just as it says: peace begins with the individual and extends to family, friends, communities, nations, the environment, and the world. If you want to learn more about peace and how you can effect it—or if you have any ideas to contribute— drop them a line. 2101 Wilshire Blvd., Santa Monica, CA 90403; 310-828-0535.

University of Santa Monica. Offers a dynamic two-year M.A. degree program in Applied Psychology, in a monthly weekend format. This practical program is on the cutting edge—where psychology meets spirituality. It is also available as a non-degree option. Approved by the State of California Dept. of Education. Write or call for a brochure. 2107 Wilshire Blvd., Santa Monica, CA 90403; 310-829-7402.

(Those organizations that would be classified as Gap-like begin here.)

Movement of Spiritual Inner Awareness (MSIA) is for those who want to live in a way that makes spirit and God a part of their lives. MSIA has no formal membership, dues, rules, or dogma. It encourages people in their own experience of the divine, without restricting personal choices. The booklet "About MSIA" describes MSIA and its goals. You can also find out if J-R's TV show, "That Which Is" is available in your area. Write or call MSIA, Box 3935, Los Angeles, CA 90051; 213-737-4055.

Discourses. John-Roger's Soul Awareness Discourses are the most complete, effective, and delightful course in Spirit I know. You simply read one a month at your own pace. Each Discourse contains about 30 pages of text and 60 blank pages for your own daily notes, reminders, dreams, discoveries, affirmations, or anything else you'd like. They're $100 per year (twelve Discourses), and I can't recommend them too highly. For more information, please contact MSIA.

Mandeville Press. Publishes J-R's earlier books, including *Relationships—The Art of Making Life Work,* and *The Power Within You.* On a more spiritual note, there's *Loving . . . Each Day, The Spiritual Promise, The Spiritual Family* and *The Way Out Book.* Other books are available. They also publish *The New Day Herald,* a bi-monthly newspaper of articles on, mostly, loving. A vast collection of John-Roger on audio and video tapes is available, looking at life from a spiritual yet practical point of view. A catalog is available from MSIA.

The LIFE 101 SERIES
by John-Roger and Peter McWilliams

LIFE 101:
Everything We Wish We Had Learned About Life In School—But Didn't

The overview book of the LIFE 101 SERIES.. The idea behind *LIFE 101* is that everyhing in life is for our upliftment, learning, and growth—including (and, perhaps, especially) the "bad" stuff. "The title jolly well says it all," said the *Los Angeles Times*—jolly well saying it all. 400 pages. **Trade paperback,** $9.95. **Audio tapes** (complete and unabridged, five cassettes), $19.95. **Wristwatch** (Paul LeBus design), $35.00.

The Portable LIFE 101

179 essential lessons from the *New York Times* bestseller *LIFE 101: Everything We Wish We Had Learned About Life In School—But Didn't.* 208 Pages. **Trade paperback,** $5.95. **Audio tape,** $9.95.

DO IT! Let's Get Off Our Buts

This is a book for those who want to discover—clearly and precisely—their dream; who choose to pursue that dream, even if it means learning (and—gasp!—practicing) some new behavior; who wouldn't mind having some fun along the way; and who are willing to expand their comfort zone enough to include their heart's desire. 500 pages. **Trade paperback,** $11.95. **Audio tapes** (complete and unabridged, six cassettes), $22.95.

The Portable DO IT!

This book contains 172 essential excerpts plus 190 quotations from the #1 *New York Times* bestseller *DO IT! Let's Get Off Our Buts.* 208 pages. **Trade paperback,** $5.95. **Audio tape,** $8.95.

You Can't Afford the Luxury of a Negative Thought

This is not just a book for people with life-threatening illnesses. It's a book for anyone afflicted with one of the primary diseases of our time: negative thinking. If, however, you have the symptoms of a life-threatening illness—be it AIDS, heart trouble, cancer, high blood pressure, or any of the others—negative thinking is a luxury you can no longer afford. 622 pages. **Trade paperback,** $14.95. **Audio tapes** (complete and unabridged, eight cassettes), $22.95. **Wristwatch** (Paul LeBus design), $35.00.

Focus on the Positive

Exercises, processes, journal space, drawing room and more—all designed to complement the preceding book. 200 pages. **Trade paperback,** $11.95.

Meditation for Loving Yourself

A beautiful meditation tape, lasting a little over half an hour. John-Roger is "backed" by a musical score composed and performed by Scott Fitzgerald and Rob Whitesides-Woo. **One cassette,** $10. This meditation tape is also included in the audio tape package of *You Can't Afford the Luxury of a Negative Thought.*

WEALTH 101: Wealth Is Much More Than Money

We define wealth as health, happiness, abundance, prosperity, riches, loving, caring, sharing, learning, knowing what we want, opportunity, enjoying, and balance. First, *WEALTH 101* explores, in detail, how to enjoy the life you already have. Then, from that foundation of appreciation and gratitude, we explore how to obtain more of what you really want. 532 pages. **Trade paperback,** $11.95. **Audio tapes** (complete and unabridged, eight cassettes), $22.95.

Meditation on Wealth

A special meditation on wealth by John-Roger, with an introduction by John Morton. **One cassette,** $10. This meditation tape is also included in the audio tape package of *WEALTH 101.*

We Give To Love: Giving Is Such a Selfish Thing Audio Tapes

The complete and unabridged text of this book, read by Academy Award nominee Sally Kirkland and Peter McWilliams. $19.95.

Other Books from Prelude Press

Ain't Nobody's Business If You Do:
The Absurdity of Consensual Crimes in a Free Society
by Peter McWilliams

What are consensual crimes? A consensual crime is any activity—currently illegal—that does not physically harm the person or property of another. The idea behind this book is simple: As an adult, you should be allowed to do with your person and property whatever you choose, as long as you don't physically harm the person or property of another. 818 pages. **Hardcover, $22.95.**

How to Survive the Loss of a Love
by Melba Colgrove, Ph.D., Harold H. Bloomfield, M.D., and Peter McWilliams

This is an entirely new edition, completely revised and updated. A directly helpful guide to recovery from any loss or major change in life. 212 pages. **Hardcover,** $10. **Trade paperback** (compact, portable size, but with full text), $5.95. **Audio tapes** (complete and unabridged, two cassettes, read by the authors), $11.95.

Surviving, Healing & Growing
The How to Survive the Loss of a Love Workbook

Exercises, processes, and suggestions designed to supplement *How to Survive the Loss of a Love.* Lots of room to write, draw, doodle, survive, heal & grow. 200 pages. **Trade paperback,** $11.95.

I Marry You Because . . .

Poetry (by Peter McWilliams) and quotations (by truly good writers) on love and marriage. 192 pages. **Trade paperback,** $5.95.

Come Love With Me & Be My Life
The Complete Romantic Poetry of Peter McWilliams

Touching, direct, emotional, often funny, the romantic poetry of Peter McWilliams has been loved by millions for the past quarter century. This is the best of his poetry. 250 pages. **Hardcover,** $12.95. **Audio tapes** (complete and unabridged, two cassettes, read by the author), $12.95.

PORTRAITS: A Book of Photographs

Many of you know Peter McWilliams's poetry from either *How to Survive the Loss of a Love* or *Come Love With Me & Be My Life*. But even before his poetry, there was photography. This is the first published collection of his photographs, focusing on portraits of people. More than thirty-five years of photography are represented. The book has a large format (9x12) and features more than 200 black & white and color photographs, exquisitely printed. 252 pages. **Hardcover,** $34.95.

To order any of these books, please check your local bookstore, or call

1-800-LIFE-101

or write to

Prelude Press
8159 Santa Monica Boulevard
Los Angeles, California 90046

Please call or write for our free catalog!

*The purpose
of getting power
is to be able
to give it away.*

ANEURIN BEVAN

Index

A

B

C

There is no cause
half so sacred
as the cause of a people.
There is no idea
so uplifting as the idea
of the service
of humanity.

WOODROW WILSON

If you would like to receive
information about future
books, tapes, lectures, etc.
by John-Roger and
Peter McWilliams,
please send
your name and address
to

Prelude Press
8159 Santa Monica Blvd.
Los Angeles, California
90046

or call
1–800–LIFE–101

Thank you.

New Yorker (victim):
"Lemme
get this straight—
you're saying that you
saw me in trouble,
so you came over
for no reason,
with nothing in it for you,
and saved my life."

Good Samaritan:
"Yep."

Victim: *"You're sick!"*

"BARNEY MILLER"

About the Authors

JOHN-ROGER, an educator, has been very busy during the past thirty years. He has traveled the world, teaching, lecturing, writing, and presenting seminars on just about every conceivable area of personal growth. He has founded several organizations dedicated to a broad range of projects including health, education, spirit, philosophy, service, integrity, corporate excellence, and individual and world peace. He has written thirty-five books, recorded hundreds of audio and video tapes, and has a nationally syndicated television show, "That Which Is."

PETER McWILLIAMS published his first book, a collection of poetry, at the age of seventeen. His series of poetry books went on to sell more than 3,500,000 copies. A book he co-authored on meditation was #1 on the *New York Times* bestseller list, as was *DO IT! Let's Get Off Our Buts.* He is the co-author of *How to Survive the Loss of a Love.* His *The Personal Computer Book* was a bestseller. His book of photographs is entitled *PORTRAITS*, and his poetry is collected in *Come Love With Me and Be My Life.* His latest book is

Ain't Nobody's Business If You Do: The Absurdity of Consensual Crimes in a Free Society. He is a nationally syndicated columnist, teaches seminars, and has appeared on the "The Oprah Winfrey Show," "Donahue," "Larry King Live" and "Today."

When the great finals come,
each one will be asked
five questions:
First:
What did you accomplish
in the world with the power
that God gave you?
Second:
How did you help
your neighbor
and what did you do
for those in need?
Third:
What did you do to serve God?
Fourth:
What did you leave
in the world
that was worth while
when you came from it?
Last:
What did you bring
into this new world
which will be of use here?

J. STANLEY DURKEE

Go give.